THE ORGANISATION SHADOW-SIDE AUDIT

William Tate
Prometheus Consulting

CSP

Cambridge Strategy Publications Ltd.
Station Offices
Station Yard
Axminster
Devon. EX13 5PF
United Kingdom

www.cambridgestrategy.com

Published in this Second Edition by:

Cambridge Strategy Publications Ltd.
An imprint of Triarchy Press Ltd.
Station Offices
Station Yard
Axminster
Devon. EX13 5PF
United Kingdom

+44 (0)1297 631456
info@cambridgestrategy.com
www.cambridgestrategy.com

First Published by Cambridge Strategy Publications Ltd. 2003

A catalogue record for this book is available from the British Library.

ISBN: 978-1-902433-97-4

Contents

FOREWORD

The Organisation Shadow-Side Audit is a business improvement tool underpinned by management development activity.

Organisations and workplaces are not rational. At best, they are clouded by petty office politics. At worst, they are crazy places, where the fog of irrationality is difficult to penetrate. In this latter type of organisation, rules and logic take second place to personal prejudices, rivalries and playing 'games'. Perhaps they always do!

The shadow-side model can be thought of as a lens through which any organisation can be seen and understood in a fresh and frank light. This self-assessment audit explains and reveals that lens. It shows how to diagnose what is happening inside your organisation, often beneath a veneer of rationality and 'spin'.

Once managers better understand the dynamics of what is going on around them, they can then analyse situations from this more informed, human perspective. They will be more streetwise, more able to take balanced decisions, and better equipped to manage complex change.

OVERVIEW

Look in any large and complex organisation. All human life is there. It would be boring - and surprising - if it wasn't. On the other hand, it needs acknowledging. It needs watching carefully. It needs understanding. It needs managing.

Yet what do most managers do when they need to make improvements in the way organisations are managed? They talk about rational things like injecting more resources and installing computers. They discuss organisation charts, mission statements, lists of competencies and tasks. They set up committees and announce new reporting channels. They devise new rules and policies. They publish edicts and make exhortations. But the organisation's problems almost certainly have more to do with such things as departmental 'turf' rivalries, personal jealousies, ambition, greed, power struggles, self-interest groups, bosses who are not on speaking terms, petty and not so petty politics, intimidation and fear. Even sexual attractions, liaisons and favours account for much of what does and doesn't get done 'according to plan'.

It is in the organisational culture and personal relationships that managers can find the most powerful clues to what's going on. Yet few managers are adept at seeing and understanding, let alone managing, this real-life scenario. It is usually beyond the bounds of training, often out of bounds completely – undiscussed and undiscussible. Yet this is the real backcloth for much of what goes on inside organisations. Organisations live and behave tabloid, but discuss and plan broadsheet.

In every kind of organisation there are things that 'go on' that are not transparent and rational; they are murky and difficult to comprehend. The dynamics are tied up in the personalities of individuals, whose actions are designed to meet their personal and sometimes dubious needs. To the 'players' these needs are more important than achieving the organisation's own legitimate goals.

Many observers find this 'game-playing' beneath contempt. They don't understand it, don't approve of it, and don't want to have any part in it. They would like to stamp it out. Yet their own behaviour is irrational, if they could but recognise it. They are blind to it and to their own and their organisation's shadow side.

Yet other people seem to take this shadow side in their stride, accepting it as part of the rich pattern of interpersonal relationships. To them, the shadow side is an inevitable part of management. Being skilful at it is key to being a successful manager. Not only do such managers understand the game and approve of it, they play it, and they play it well. Some positively revel in it; it is the whole point of work.

Whatever you think of the shadow side, there is no denying that it is pervasive in organisations. But it can also be viewed as necessary. Organisations need their shadow side as a kind of safety valve. Exploiting the shadow side can be seen as honourable. Far from making the workplace less effective, this perspective argues that the shadow side is where we retain our individuality and humanity against the pressures of our formal roles and the organisation's requirements and rules. If you accept this notion, then the task of management is not to tame the shadow side, but to sustain it in a state of balance alongside the official system.

Managing the shadow side might sound like a 'promotional' for *The Prince,* Niccolò Machiavelli's classic description of power and manipulation. But that is not our motivation here; quite the opposite. While some of the illustrations in the text show managers using the shadow side for personal gain, our intention is to show how to manage the shadow side to benefit the organisation.

Failure to do this entails a major human and economic cost. When things go wrong, managers often seek comfort in blaming 'human error'. They remain blind to shortcomings in the system (for example, fatal hospital errors such as the injection of wrong drugs). Yet the reverse is also common. Managers frequently seek rational solutions, such as new structures, rules and edicts, while neglecting human nature.

Managing the shadow side means achieving a fine balance between the rational and non-rational. This audit shows how that is possible. It approaches the subject at various levels:

- Understanding what the shadow side is: the models and elements that comprise it.
- Why the shadow side matters in organisations, and why it is important to gain control over it.
- Developing more highly tuned personal antennae that give you the ability to see the shadow side at work.
- Acquiring the analytical skill to be able to tease out just what is going on at any time.
- Improving your skills in managing the shadow side and managing yourself better in that environment.
- Bringing benefits to your organisation in everyday performance and especially at times of change.

BUSINESS BENEFITS

By undertaking this self-assessment you will:-

1. Obtain a clear understanding of the nature of the shadow side of organisational life and its potency.

2. Develop a balanced perspective of the shadow side, both its positive and negative attributes.

3. Hone your antennae and sharpen your ability to detect where the shadow side is responsible for particular situations you are experiencing.

4. Discover how to bring awkward and sensitive issues out of the shadows, enabling important but previously undiscussed matters to become discussible and manageable.

5. Develop skills attuned to the demands that the shadow side places on managers and where you need to make a well-informed contribution that matches the game being played.

6. Know what you are getting yourself into and be less likely to be deceived by action or data designed to please you.

7. Take more rounded decisions.

8. Find it easier to gain acceptance for your proposals.

9. Choose wisely where to commit your effort and resources.

10. Gain a reputation for being more streetwise.

As a result, your organisation will:

11. Establish a more open culture.

12. Improve interpersonal relationships.

13. Engage in more honest and open dialogue.

14. Find problems are brought to the surface with confidence and are more easily resolved.

15. Be more successful at managing change.

16. Establish a baseline from which to audit the shadow side at a future date and measure progress.

ABOUT CAMBRIDGE STRATEGY AUDITS

Concept

- A Cambridge Strategy self-assessment audit is broader in scope than the traditional company audit which concentrates on verifying figures and checking whether suitable control processes are in place and working. Cambridge Strategy audits concern the full spectrum of management activity – tangible and intangible – with a bias towards the people side of the organisation.

- The audits look at what you (as an organisation) are doing and what you are not doing. They look for gaps in your practice, as well as evaluating how well various policies, processes and programmes are working. We use the term 'audit' to mean assessing, checking, evaluating and improving. Our audits combine a gap analysis and health check with improvement advice. The process is designed to help you think, compare, illuminate, learn, plan and improve.

- The audits are not prescriptive. They do not propose one-size-fits-all solutions. They acknowledge that significant differences in needs and traditions exist between individual companies. Every organisation is unique and must be free to adapt best practice and ideas to its own context and circumstances. We also recognise differences between sectors. For example, circumstances in the professions and in the public sector are different from the private sector – though there are signs of convergence.

- Cambridge Strategy audits are all self-assessments. You take responsibility for carrying out the audit yourself in your own area of activity. You know the results and you decide what to do about them. This is different from the types of audit conducted by people from an external perspective to check, approve and certify.

- Ultimately, what matters to companies is success at the level of the overall business. By the 'business' we mean the outward-facing view on markets, products, customers, outlets, orders, sales, competitors, margins, profits and so on (and their public sector equivalent). To achieve such business success requires an organisation behind it, well designed and run to serve the needs of the chosen business efficiently and effectively. It is this 'internal organisation' that is the focus of most management activity. So our audits focus mainly on this 'internal organisation'; i.e. they are more concerned with the *enablers* of results than the ultimate business *results* themselves. Put another way, the audits examine the internal organisation's inputs, throughputs and outputs, more than the outcomes and benefits. They concentrate on means more than ends.

- Each audit theme comprises two main components. There is first a descriptive part or 'learning input', containing a definition, discussion, explanation and advice on the particular theme. This is immediately followed by the next component: a questionnaire. The questionnaire enables you to assess your own organisation. It helps you to measure your current performance in each theme's subject area and identify the gaps and scope for improvement. The use of the questionnaires is explained at this point.

- The questionnaires rely heavily on numbers for scoring. But many of the issues considered are inherently qualitative not quantitative. As such, they don't naturally lend themselves to numbers. This mirrors management. Many of the most important things in organisations, as in life, cannot be measured easily and accurately. In using numbers, we are not advocating management by numbers or numerical targets. Even if figures are accurate, they still call for interpretation, judgement, common sense, imagination and intuition. Besides, auditing is not the same as managing. But scoring the questionnaires in this way does enable us to measure and track the improvement process.

Who the audits are for

Cambridge Strategy audits are designed for senior managers in sophisticated organisations – usually medium to large. Areas covered by individual audits typically include HR, marketing, public relations, quality, finance, etc.

The Organisation Shadow-Side Audit is designed for those with responsibility for ensuring that their organisation's aims and objectives stand the best possible chance of being met.

This audit is designed and written for directors of HR, training, and management/ organisation development, organisation learning and knowledge management. Depending on the size and nature of the organisation, it may also be used by chief executives, managing directors and chief operating officers. If not personally involved in conducting the audit, then, at the very least, top management should sponsor and support use of the audit and take part in discussions on the findings and proposed improvement action.

Ways of undertaking the audit

The audit can be worked through in a number of ways:

1. After reading about the themes, a group sits round a table and discusses and scores each one in turn. Someone records the consensus.

2. Several individuals complete questionnaires in parallel and then discuss their separate results.

3. Individuals complete the audit on their own and then discuss and refine their different results with colleagues.

4. Individuals complete the audit on their own.

Considerable benefit is derived from discussing and reconciling different perceptions and ideas. Whichever of the above options is chosen, users will normally want to share with colleagues their ideas for taking subsequent improvement action.

Facilitated workshops

The audits are designed as stand alone self-assessment tools and can be used immediately to add value to the way your organisation is run. But, where possible, workshops are a good way of augmenting the learning process, because they help you:

- amplify on the learning element
- complete the questionnaires under guidance
- share data with the facilitator and other participants
- build upon the questionnaire results
- benchmark the results
- discuss ideas for taking improvement action

Workshops are also a useful way of involving a wider group in the planning process by enabling managers to step outside the daily operational system and view matters strategically from an objective perspective.

Good luck!

Our audits are a very satisfying and powerful way to start improving your organisation. We wish you every success in using them. Please give us feedback so that we can improve them. And let us know if you need any further support.

AN INTRODUCTION TO THE SHADOW SIDE

Most readers will be familiar with the idea that there is a shadow side in human personality. When thinking negatively we may speak of it as the 'dark side'. We associate it with 'bad' people. But each of us has a side that is not rational and may be less than wholesome. There are things that we don't admit to others, maybe not even to ourselves. We prefer to keep these habits, behaviours, thoughts, beliefs, prejudices, fantasies, vices and ideas hidden in the shadows.

In this audit the shadow side is the organisational equivalent of the shadow side in human personality. Since organisations comprise individuals, the organisation's shadow side inevitably reflects much that is inherent in human personality – in leaders, managers and employees. But there is much more to an organisation's shadow side than the vagaries of individuals. Indeed, some aspects of the shadow side are positive, by no means tainted, inadmissible and unworthy. Just as the shadow side is inevitable in any organisation, arguably it is also necessary.

Some organisation psychologists have made a study of the subject. Here we briefly explain their views. Their models contain both individual and organisational behavioural components. Where the behaviour is classically associated with individuals (e.g. greed), then the models are concerned with the organisational causes and consequences of this attribute. But besides such individual aspects, the organisation has direct shadow-side component features of its own, especially in its culture. One such popular model is advanced by Gerard Egan, and this informs many of the audit's themes. His definition of the shadow side is:

> *All those things that substantially and consistently affect the productivity and quality of the working life of a business, for better or worse, but which are not found on organisational charts, in company manuals, or in the discussions that take place in formal meetings.*

A slightly different model is espoused by Trevor Bentley, a Gestalt psychologist. Bentley's model is more obviously an organisational model, less based on individual personality and behaviour. This model emphasises the wholeness of the two complementary sides – the legitimate and the shadow. It stresses the virtues of the shadow side more strongly than does Egan's. Bentley's work shares much in common with that of Ralph Stacey, a prominent writer on complexity and chaos theory. While considering the shadow side as 'vital', Stacey also views the two sides as 'enemies'. His definition is:

> *The set of interactions among members of a legitimate system that fall outside that legitimate system. It comprises all social and political interactions that are outside the rules strictly prescribed by the legitimate system. It is the arena in which members of an organisation pursue their own gain…*

All models speak of two systems in any organisation, but use slightly different terms. Egan speaks of the rational side versus the non-rational (i.e. shadow side). Bentley talks about the legitimate system and the shadow system. Alongside the legitimate system Stacey talks about both the shadow system and also shadow networks.

In this audit the descriptions of different models, and comparisons between them, are the audit author's own. In places, they have been extended or adapted to suit the selfassessment process. For a full account of the models, see the original works (listed in the *References* section).

The rational and non-rational

The rational half of organisational life is concerned with how managers prefer to think and talk about the organisation; for example, how job roles fit together, and therefore how (at least on paper) work is assumed to get done. But this is not what in reality makes the organisation tick. To get the fuller picture one must be aware of the non-rational half. To give a 'taster' here are some examples:

TABLE 1
ELEMENTS OF THE TWO SIDES

Rational elements	Non-rational (shadow side) elements
• Directives	• Trust
• Strategic plans	• Friendships
• Organisation charts	• Jealousy
• Job titles	• Fear and insecurity
• Policies	• Power struggles
• Training courses	• Ambition
• Budgets	• Grapevine

Egan uses the term *non-rational* (and sometimes 'arational') as opposed to *irrational*. He views the effect that these factors collectively have on the health of the organisation as a mix of positive, negative and neutral. Thus, friendships, for example, are not rational or logical features of an organisation. Neither are they irrational. Their impact may be positive, negative or neutral, or a mix of these at different times. For example, friendships can be the means of getting round obstructions and bureaucracy.

It is commonly accepted that the two halves of the human brain perform different functions. The left hemisphere processes rational thinking, numbers etc, while the right hemisphere handles colour, music, intuition, and so on. Based on this analogy, and as a way of gaining understanding of the shadow-side concept, we can liken the two sides of an organisation to the left and right brain hemispheres, giving them the broadly differentiated characteristics shown below.

TABLE 2
THE CHARACTER OF THE TWO SIDES

Rational characteristics (left brain)	Non-rational (shadow side) characteristics (right brain)
• What is intended to happen	• What really happens
• Things	• People
• What	• Who
• Logical/thinking	• Emotional/feeling
• Overt	• Covert
• Discussed	• Undiscussed

The rational factors are generally more explicit. They are usually written down, and they tend to deal with 'what' issues. By contrast, shadow-side factors are generally implicit and are more likely to concern 'who' issues. Table 3 gives a fuller list of the factors that comprise the two sides.

TABLE 3
EXTENDED LIST OF ELEMENTS IN THE TWO HALVES OF ORGANISATIONAL LIFE

Rational factors	Non-rational (shadow-side) factors
• announcements	• culture
• edicts	• climate
• directives	• values and beliefs
• exhortation	• ethics
• mission	• norms, custom and practice
• goals	• myths
• objectives	• personal rivalries
• targets	• departmental rivalries
• strategies	• territorial ('turf') disputes
• policies	• power struggles
• systems	• empire-building
• statistics	• competition/collaboration
• databases	• personal jealousies and envy
• plans	• biases and prejudices
• standing instructions	• office politics
• company rules and regulations	• ambition
• codes of practice/ethics	• greed
• statements of business principles	• self-interest
• credos	• hopes and aspirations
• organisation charts/structure	• trust
• budgets	• respect
• sign-off authority levels	• fear and insecurity
• contracts	• turning a blind eye
• laws and statutes	• personal friendships
• job descriptions	• sexual relationships and attraction
• job titles	• socialising
• published policies	• networking
• committee structures	• short cuts
• qualifications	• expediency
• skills, knowledge	• group-think
• lists of competencies	• bosses not on speaking terms
• appraisal procedures	• in-groups and out-groups
• pay structure	• grapevine
• training courses	• bullying and intimidation
• office standards (e.g. dress)	• stress
	• personal appearance
	• favours
	• bribes and back-handers
	• horse-trading
	• industrial surveillance
	• industrial sabotage
	• ploys

Extract from William Tate: *Demerging Organisations,* Financial Times Management, Pearson Education, 1999

Note how seldom items in the right-hand column find a place on the boardroom agenda, despite their potency. Note too how most shadow-side elements are the kind of behaviour and drives that we associate most naturally with individuals. But a few are direct organisation manifestations: for example, the organisation's culture, customs and norms, departmental rivalries, and the grapevine.

From this list it is easy to see how an organisation in which the shadow-side variables are dominant might be chaotic or anarchic. On the other hand, if these are strongly suppressed, the organisation might be too restrictive, predictable and unimaginative. Hence the idea that these two sides of the organisation form an equation, with some kind of balance needing to exist between them.

The balance of power and influence that one side has vis-à-vis the other varies between organisations. Some workplaces are fairly straightforward, predictable, easy to fathom and possible to manage. Others remain a mystery, are 'crazy' and difficult to manage unless you understand the idiosyncratic rules and have well-honed political skills.

Managed chaos

Bentley and Stacey regard balancing the two sides of the organisation as important and needing active management. According to Bentley, the essential characteristics are as shown below.

The legitimate system	The shadow system
• Organised by those in authority.	• Self-organising.
	• Obscure.
	• Serves people's personal needs.
	• Welcomes diversity.
	• Supports people in being who they are rather than how the organisation needs them to be.
• People usually contract and conform.	• People usually expand and blossom.
• Change initiatives target the legitimate system.	• Change initiatives require the support of the shadow system.

This model places considerable value in the shadow system. It serves as a natural safety valve where people can take care of themselves against the rigours of their formal roles. Managers need to understand its nature and maintain it as a kind of semi-legitimate counterweight to the official legitimate system.

The shadow system initially appears dysfunctional. It runs counter to a single system that is rational and focused entirely on serving the organisation's legitimate purpose. But Stacey points out that:

People do not come together in organizations simply to perform primary tasks. While they work they also socialize with each other to form a shadow system. They may use this system to sabotage the primary task or to constitute a learning community that assists the legitimate system to function in the face of ambiguity and uncertainty by circumventing its rules.

Brief examples of the shadow side

Here are some quick and easy 'tasters' to give a feel for the shadow side:

The prophet without honour

An internal consultant – however capable – lacks the credibility of an external consultant. The higher the fee rate, the greater the credibility. And once you, as client, are committed to paying for advice, you feel almost bound to say you like the recommended solution. Otherwise, it reflects badly on your own earlier decision.

FAILED PROPHETS

A large company asked its own internal consulting department to work on organisation problems. A particular problem had a long history, which had defied attempts to solve it internally. At last there was a breakthrough, and the head of internal consulting sought an urgent meeting with the chief executive, but was rebuffed repeatedly because of time pressures in the chief executive's diary. Then the chief executive hired external consultants. A key meeting between the chief executive and the firm of consultants was scheduled over breakfast time. The head of internal consulting was invited to attend and found himself sitting next to the outside firm's lead consultant. When the chief executive asked the lead consultant what he would recommend, the exasperated but loyal internal consultant wrote his solution on his companion's napkin, who promptly 'sold' the solution to the chief executive.

Familiarity breeds contempt

Attempts at false familiarity can backfire:

ONE OF THE LADS

A particular chief executive, when taking important VIPs on a tour of his company, would call everyone he encountered by their first name. This impressed the VIPs. One expressed her surprise and delight to a shop-floor member of staff, who quietly informed her that an order had gone out to everyone that the boss would call you by some fictitious first name and you were not to point out that this was not actually your real name.

Passing the buck

When a new boss inherits a shambles, it pays to paint as black as picture as possible quickly, bring forward costs and load these into the current year, and make all the bad news stick to the previous incumbent. The contrast between the two regimes' figures is then more impressive.

Softening up the opposition

Shadow-side tactics can be useful in getting a proposal agreed.

> SLIPPING ONE THROUGH
>
> **The directors of a German subsidiary of Redland, once a top FTSE 100 company (taken over by Lafarge in the mid-1990s), were suspicious of Redland's close ties to City of London investment bankers. They feared Redland would take all their German money and give it to the City. When the Germans needed the Redland Board to endorse an important but controversial strategy, they first put forward a series of ridiculous propositions and let Redland win the argument in rejecting each one. Once the softening up was complete, the subsidiary's directors put forward their serious proposal and it went through on the nod.**

Queueing

Queues are not always what they seem. Shortening them is not always what managers want (though it may be what they and their organisation need).

> QUEUEING THEORY
>
> **A UK management consultant working with a Kuwaiti company offered to help a manager reduce the length of queues of employees outside his office. The manager explained to the consultant that reducing the queue was the last thing he wanted. The length of the queue was a measure of his importance. Queues were an important status symbol.**

While aspects of the shadow side are universal (e.g. the need for personal status), their realisation may be culturally determined, as with the queuing example where productivity and efficiency (of the manager and of those queuing) was not paramount.

Can the shadow side be managed?

Suggesting that an organisation's shadow side might be a serious subject for study and managerial skill development may encounter a range of responses:

> "There's nothing you can do about this kind of thing. You just have to learn to live with it."

> "We know all about that already. What's the big deal? It's just part of being savvy."
>
> "How can I learn to better manage my way through the shadow side in order to survive and get things done?"
>
> "As a senior manager responsible for the way the organisation works, how can I gain a degree of control over the excesses of the shadow side, and make the organisation work more rationally?"

There's truth and merit in all these responses, including the sceptical ones. Some manifestations of the shadow side are probably out of reach of all but the most patient, forgiving and imaginative. But this audit aims to make managing the shadow side seem an obvious candidate for legitimate and practical study.

ABOUT THE QUESTIONNAIRES

Using the questionnaires

Some questions ask you to state your organisation's position on an item. In instances where that is bound to be a matter of opinion, a question will ask you to state your own view on the organisation's position (or you may wish to establish a group view – see below). Other questions ask you to state your own personal position on an item as it applies to you. Each question should make the context clear.

The audit's assessment process is designed primarily to highlight implications for the organisation and the way it is managed. However, some of the personal questions, and the way you answer them, may hold implications for your own learning and development. The more senior and influential you are in the organisation, the greater will be the organisational consequences of your own personal assessment and learning.

There may be some questions you cannot answer immediately and where you will need to seek factual information from someone with the necessary information or expertise. Some questions also ask for perceptions of current practice. There may be benefit in convening a group to elicit these perceptions.

If the wording of questions doesn't exactly match your circumstances, please amend or interpret them in a way that is most relevant and helpful.

Questions are scored using a four-point scale (0, 1, 2, 3), plus 'don't know'. A score of three is generally the most favourable (but see the note at the start of Questionnaire 1). You can add up your score at the end of each section and use it for any of the purposes described earlier. Note that in some questions the score 0 – 3 is reversed.

You may choose to assess your whole organisation, a departmental unit, or a geographical division, as appropriate.

Each questionnaire covers a single theme. Any one may be used on its own if a particular focus is wanted. However, the overall set is designed in an integrated and comprehensive way. Full benefit is gained from working through all ten questionnaires.

The scoring options

You may choose to undertake the overall assessment in one session or over several sittings, with time to reflect between.

You may consider asking colleagues to score copies of the questionnaire and then compare and discuss results. Or you can discuss each question in turn and for the organisational items agree a consensus score. You might also like to share scores on personal items, but there is no need to seek a consensus. These are all powerful ways to learn.

The design of questions

The wording of the questions is designed to make the ideal answer obvious. They are not jumbled to confuse or disguise good practice.

Recording and monitoring assessment

After completion transfer the totals to the overall score sheet (below). Where a theme's score distinguishes between your organisation and you personally, you may wish to show both scores.

	Score 1st Time	Score 2nd Time
1. Office politics		
2. Trust and relationships		
3. Training and development		
4. Creativity and innovation		
5. Reward and punishment		
6. Target setting		
7. Management by numbers		
8. Change management		
9. Organisation culture		
Aggregate score		
Percentage	%	%

Using the results

You can use the scores to:

1. Share different perceptions, comparing your own score with the score of others in your organisation who have undertaken the audit questions separately.
2. Decide where the greatest weaknesses are and which themes should be given the highest priority for improvement.
3. Decide how much and how urgently you need to take improvement action. For scored items, an average of less than two (out of a maximum of four) suggests significant scope exists for improvement.
4. Compare your progress over time. You can re-score the item at regular intervals (e.g. annually).
5. Check the effectiveness of your improvements by scoring items before and after you have taken action.
6. Benchmark yourself against others that have agreed to share their scores. This might be different divisions or sites within an organisation, or different organisations.

Ways of applying the results to gain benefits include:

1. Pinpointing problems that need fixing quickly.
2. Facilitating an exchange of views with colleagues about problems, opportunities and improvement plans.
3. Triggering imaginative improvement action.
4. 'Selling' controversial improvement action and obtaining buy-in.
5. Co-ordinating improvement action across HR disciplines.
6. Designing more relevant development programmes, schemes and courses.
7. Giving individual learners direction and meaning to their personal development.

Interpreting your score

Your score will give you a feel for where your organisation currently stands against generally accepted best practice. You can do this within each of the themes and then make comparisons across the areas.

Your score will help you monitor your organisation's progress over time as you introduce changes.

If you score less than 50% you may wish to seek advice on how to make improvements. You may contact the author or the publisher (see appendices).

Copying the questionnaires

Each questionnaire is preceded by related 'learning input'. After reading this, you will then find the relevant questionnaire. You may choose to complete each questionnaire right away while things are fresh in your mind, before you move on to the next theme. If you prefer you can of course leave all the questionnaires until later or until you have read all nine themes.

It is a good idea to photocopy the questionnaires when you first come to them so you can distribute them to your colleagues if you wish.

The purchase price and copyright agreement contains a photocopy licence. This allows you to copy the questionnaire pages, before and/or after completing them, for the purpose of sharing learning. It does not entitle you to photocopy the whole document. To buy a photocopying agreement that entitles you to produce multiple copies of the complete audit, or to buy further printed copies at a bulk purchase discount price, or to buy a pdf copy of this entire audit, or to order (free of charge to customers) a pdf copy of the questionnaires, please contact the publisher (see appendix for details).

MANAGING THE SHADOW SIDE: THE NINE THEMES

1. Office politics
This is the aspect most people first think of when considering the shadow side. It may be their only one. Everyone has a negative story to tell about office politics. Yet there is a positive side. How can managers learn how to use 'positive politics'?

2. Trust and relationships
Trust lies at the heart of quality relationships and dialogue. It affects what can and cannot be discussed, and what cannot even be mentioned as a possible subject for discussion. It influences what gets openly shared and reported, what gets covered up. What can be voiced without fear?

3. Training and development
Training is often blamed when the public spotlight is turned on organisation mishaps, but then claimed to have magic power to provide solutions. Hence trainers frequently get caught up in machinations. How can training do an honest job?

4. Creativity and innovation
Creative people and new ideas exist at the boundary of what's comfortably tolerated by an organisation. They threaten the status quo and pose a challenge to the formal, legitimate system. How can organisations optimise their innovating potential?

5. Reward and punishment
Managers try to align their organisation systems with what they suppose are individuals' needs and motivations, including greed and status, as well as exhibiting their own need to display power and dominance. How can rewards be used honourably to help the business?

6. Target setting
Targets are popular with those who set them, and unpopular with those on the receiving end. They are the source of endless political games and diversions from the real business that the targets are intended to improve. How can targets be used soundly and acceptably?

7. Management by numbers
The days of reducing managerial success to numbers is gone. Yet number-crunchers still fall victim to the charm of numbers, besides abusing them as "Lies, damned lies and statistics". How can we see numbers clearly for what they are and use them honestly and wisely?

8. Change management

The destabilising turmoil of change, or mere threat of it, invokes shadow-side responses from many. How can those who manage change try to plan and design it in a way that recognises how human nature affects its likelihood of success?

9. Organisation culture

Culture is the source of the values, beliefs and norms that underpin many of the manifestations of the shadow side in an organisation. It determines 'how crazy it is round here' and whether people collaborate or compete. In your organisation does rationality or irrationality prevail?

THEME 1: OFFICE POLITICS

Everyone who works in an organisation has a gripe about office politics (or 'micropolitical behaviour' as it is more correctly called). 'Politics' is the most familiar, most discussed and best understood of the elements that comprise an organisation's shadow side. Even those who are prime exponents of the art of politics complain about it. Politics is often considered endemic and a fact of life. Many people believe that you just have to learn to live with it. Not true! But first, what is 'it'?

Political behaviour

Two sets of examples are shown below:

- manipulation
- manoeuvring
- string-pulling
- game playing
- back-stabbing
- bitching
- buck-passing
- bullying
- sucking up
- stamping down
- claiming success
- stitching up
- making yourself look good
- getting the lion's share of power
- and glory

Extract from Karen Lee: 'Coping with Office Politics', *Consulting into the Future,* Management Consultancies Association, 2002

- networking to build a power base
- grasping opportunities to increase
- visibility
- burying unfavourable information
- withholding information from rivals
- scapegoating to avoid personal blame
- taking credit for others' success

Extract from Linda Holbeche: *Politics in Organisations,* Roffey Park Management Institute, 2002

Organisation consequences

Given these descriptions, it is not surprising that 'playing politics' is nearly always viewed negatively and is practised covertly outside the official system. Many people believe that political behaviour reduces organisational effectiveness and productivity. Holbeche asserts that politics:

- create a lack of trust
- reduce morale

- exclude key people from decision-making processes
- reduce faith in top management
- increase internal competition and conflict
- hamper knowledge sharing
- prevent merit from being rewarded
- lead to the loss of talent

Power and favouritism

Inevitably, unofficial politics are played within the world of official Politics. They usually concern favouritism and/or power. In one such instance, revelations about the lives of UK Government spin-doctors shed light into the murky depths of the civil service. The sacking of Jo Moore, special adviser ('spin doctor') to Stephen Byers, then Secretary of State for the Department for Transport, Local Government and the Regions, blighted a number of promising careers.

SPIN DOCTORS

The report by the Public Administration Select Committee concluded that "internal warfare had ripped his [i.e. Byers'] department apart and that normal controls were unable to cope with Jo Moore ... Ms Moore had been an 'unusually active' special adviser, who had assumed 'executive' and 'management' tasks 'without reference to proper procedures'. ... Ms Moore, who prompted a crisis after she sent an email claiming that 11 September was a good day to bury bad news, was beyond dismissal by Sir Richard Mottram, the Permanent Secretary, because of her close political relationship with Stephen Byers. ... a perception in Whitehall that there was one law for the special advisers and one law for the rest. ... 'Internal war' had gripped the department and the system could not cope. ... Career civil servants, gripped by a sense of unfairness, took the law into their own hands by leaking to the media.

Extract from 'MPs demand safeguards to stop bullying spin doctors', *The Independent,* 19 July 2002

Frustration built up over Ms Moore's behaviour to the point where other frustrated, and perhaps jealous, civil servants blew the whistle on what was going on. Lacking an official means for letting off steam and achieving a desired result (i.e. Ms Moore's dismissal), they too breached procedures and 'leaked' information to the press – one of the spin doctors' own tricks. Paradoxically, the job of spin doctoring is a form of official shadow-side activity. Perhaps it is poetic justice that 'those who live by the sword die by the sword'.

Positive politics

Whether or not politics is as negative as portrayed in the last example, it is clearly an important facet of organisational life. Managers cannot afford to deny or ignore politics. Better they join the club and acquire and practise political skills. That is merely being pragmatic. But, going a step further, politics can be viewed in an honourable light. There are two kinds of politics – the politics of self-interest and politics designed to serve the best interests of the organisation (positive politics).

While much that is wrong in organisations gets blamed on "politics", arguably it is a legitimate target for positive managing. Much politicking is petty, but serious politics is the means of marshalling scarce resources and support in order to get important things done. Positive politics can serve the needs of the organisation.

There is a finite amount of energy, finance, and time available in organisations. People with ideas that they genuinely believe are for the good of the organisation must learn how to manage the political system in order to attract the maximum support. Lobbying, trading favours, forming alliances, and flattery are all legitimate weapons in the politician's armoury.

Political strategies

Whether political behaviour is positive or negative is largely a matter of intent. The behaviour may be similar, but good politics is underpinned by good intentions. By that we mean that the hoped-for outcome is assumed to serve the organisation's interests (though it will usually serve the manager's own ends too.)

To survive in a political landscape, the following strategies are helpful:-

TABLE 4 POLITICAL STRATEGIES
• Learn the name of the game. • Identify those who have political influence. • Identify the interests of the key players and meet them. • Determine the most effective channels of communication. • Mobilise support for your ideas. • Anticipate the strategies that others are most likely to employ. • Blend other people's needs with your own. • Establish and use informal communication networks. • Enter into alliances and form coalitions. • Know who 'owes you one'. • Learn how to use trade-offs well. • Maximise flexibility without becoming slippery. • Balance overt and covert action.

Types of political skill

You can use the chart below to analyse yourself as a politician. The matrix categorises people into four basic types depending on their motives or intentions and their skill or competence.

FIGURE 1
POLITICAL TYPES

	COMPETENCE Low	COMPETENCE High
MOTIVES: Honourable	2	1
MOTIVES: Self-serving	4	3

1. People in this category possess the political skill to operate effectively in an organisation context.

2. These people are well-intentioned, but lack the political skill to achieve their objectives; they may be perceived as naïve, irritants, innocents, militants or wellmeaning incompetents.

3. People here may be perceived as Machiavellian (after Niccolò Machiavelli's *The Prince)*. The category covers those whose motives are suspect and who are adept at understanding and interpreting situations, and making what they want to happen.

4. People in this group may be prone to misjudging situations or acting in a way that is transparently self-seeking and less effective.

Theme 1 Questionnaire: Are you a Match for the Politics in your Organisation?

ASSESSMENT

Write in empty boxes, complete statements, circle options, or tick where applicable. Numbers equate to points scored.

NB: A political organisation is a reality. Your scores on the rating scales below will indicate how political your organisation is, not whether the politics are good or bad. You can then compare your political skills with these realities. You may, however, additionally conclude that high scores on certain items within a high overall score for your organisation are a source of concern.

In your organisation

1.1 How significant are politics in the life and culture of your organisation?
Don't know | 0. Not at all | 1. A little | 2. Fairly | 3. Very

1.2 Do the important decisions in your organisation get decided through informal channels more than formal ones?
Don't know | 0. Not at all | 1. A little | 2. Fairly | 3. Very

1.3 How negative is the politicking?
Don't know | 0. Not at all | 1. A little | 2. Fairly | 3. Very

1.4 Are conflicts of interest frequent?
Don't know | 0. Not at all | 1. A little | 2. Fairly | 3. Very

1.5 Are personality conflicts frequent?
Don't know | 0. Not at all | 1. A little | 2. Fairly | 3. Very

1.6 Are ideological conflicts frequent?
Don't know | 0. Not at all | 1. A little | 2. Fairly | 3. Very

1.7 Are structural conflicts frequent?
Don't know | 0. Not at all | 1. A little | 2. Fairly | 3. Very

1.8 Are conflicts over funds frequent?
Don't know | 0. Not at all | 1. A little | 2. Fairly | 3. Very

1.9 Are conflicts over talent frequent?
Don't know | 0. Not at all | 1. A little | 2. Fairly | 3. Very

1.10 How internally competitive is the culture?
Don't know | 0. Not at all | 1. A little | 2. Fairly | 3. Very

1.11	How limited are financial resources?				
	Don't know	0. Not at all	1. A little	2. Fairly	3. Very
1.12	How limited are human resources?				
	Don't know	0. Not at all	1. A little	2. Fairly	3. Very
1.13	How pervasive is punishment?				
	Don't know	0. Not at all	1. A little	2. Fairly	3. Very
1.14	How high are the rewards for success?				
	Don't know	0. Not at all	1. A little	2. Fairly	3. Very
1.15	Does who you know matter more than what you know?				
	Don't know	0. Not at all	1. A little	2. Fairly	3. Very
1.16	How much is the organisation involved in change?				
	Don't know	0. Not at all	1. A little	2. Fairly	3. Very
1.17	How unclear is the organisation about its values?				
	Don't know	0. Not at all	1. A little	2. Fairly	3. Very
1.18	Does the organisation fail to live up to its stated values?				
	Don't know	0. Not at all	1. A little	2. Fairly	3. Very

You personally

1.19	Do you personally have the level of influence that your job position merits?				
	Don't know	0. Not at all	1. A little	2. Fairly	3. Very
1.20	Do you get the budget that your responsibilities need?				
	Don't know	0. Not at all	1. A little	2. Fairly	3. Very
1.21	Do you feel well informed about what is going on around you?				
	Don't know	0. Not at all	1. A little	2. Fairly	3. Very
1.22	Do you use informal channels to influence things in a way that favours you?				
	Don't know	0. Not at all	1. A little	2. Fairly	3. Very
1.23	How important do you consider making your boss feel good?				
	Don't know	0. Not at all	1. A little	2. Fairly	3. Very
1.24	How adept are you at making your boss feel good?				
	Don't know	0. Not at all	1. A little	2. Fairly	3. Very
1.25	How aware are you of the important cliques to which you need to belong?				
	Don't know	0. Not at all	1. A little	2. Fairly	3. Very

1.26

How strong is your membership of the important cliques?				
Don't know	0. Not at all	1. A little	2. Fairly	3. Very
To which cliques do you need to gain membership?				

1.27

How aware are you of where you need to build better relationships?				
Don't know	0. Not at all	1. A little	2. Fairly	3. Very
Which relationships do you most need to improve?				

1.28

How good a political role model are you?				
Don't know	0. Not at all	1. A little	2. Fairly	3. Very
Who are the political role models you would most like to emulate?				

1.29

Using the matrix of 'political types' in Figure 1, which type are you?			
Type 1	Type 2	Type 3	Type 4
☐	☐	☐	☐
3	1	1	0

1.30

Of the political behaviours listed earlier, which are you pleased about in yourself and which are you ashamed of?	
Pleased about:	Ashamed of:

SCORING

Your organisation			**Yourself**		
Total number of points scored	☐		Total number of points scored	☐	
Out of a possible maximum of	54		Out of a possible maximum of	33	
Percentage =	☐	%	Percentage =	☐	%

By comparing the two percentage scores (for your organisation and yourself) you can measure your level of political skill relative to the demands for that skill.

THEME 1: OFFICE POLITICS

REFLECTIONS

Capture your observations, thoughts and ideas here.

Good ideas that I have picked up:

Important things that my organisation should do:

Urgent things that my organisation should do:

Things that I can and should do myself:

Things that I need to investigate further:

Things that I need to discuss with other people (say whom):

THEME 2: TRUST AND RELATIONSHIPS

Trustful relationships

Trust is vital in any organisation. It is part of the glue that holds relationships between individuals and between departments together. Trust is the basis of delegation, whether on the giving or receiving end. Trust works both ways: top managers have to be trusted too.

At the top of companies, managers need to trust the motives and direction of their board. Investors of capital need to trust their agents (the board directors) to act in their interest. Wider groups of stakeholders, include society in general, need to be able to trust a business, otherwise it may lose its tacit 'licence to operate'. Employees need to be able to trust their directors to safeguard their interests and not line their own pockets at the expense of other groups.

But trust is not regularly discussed at board meetings. Trust is not usually referred to in policy documents, charts or descriptions of how the organisation is meant to work. That is changing, however, as interest grows in publishing statements of business principles, codes of conduct, and corporate values.

Trusting types

Trust can mean many different things. One may be trusted by one's boss, colleagues, staff or customers. And that trust is manifested in many ways. When people speak of trust they usually mean more than simple honesty. Among other things, a person may be trusted to:

- share the company's aims
- safeguard the company's assets
- maintain a confidence
- have sound judgement
- work late when needed
- deliver results on time
- give honest feedback
- not let the team down
- not 'rat' on workmates
- report on corrupt practices
- not take unacceptable short-cuts
- not endanger self or others
- suggest improvements in how work gets done

'Trust' features in most climate surveys which companies use to establish the mood of their employees. If you are conducting a survey in your own company, be sure everyone is clear what you mean by trust. Give the term 'action' by saying who does what to whom. Without this, *you* may be clear what you mean, but others may think you mean something else. Together you may not even know you are talking about quite different things.

Mergers and demergers

Mergers and demergers provide a rich seam for students of the shadow side to mine. As with any major organisational change, trust is paramount.

The demerger of the Burton Group in order to separate the Debenhams department store from what became Arcadia, the high street multiples business, provides an interesting, though commonplace, example of interpersonal trust.

> *An important question in getting things done during the demerger was: 'Who has the ear of John Hoerner?' [Arcadia's then chief executive] 'Whom does he trust, like and listen to?' That person would then be chosen to seek to persuade him.*
>
> (Extract from William Tate: *Demerging Organisations: A Guide to Best Practice.* Financial Times Management, Pearson Education 1999)

The demerger of Tarmac in 1999 showed a breakdown of trust between the board and its institutional investors.

TARMAC

Construction group Tarmac faces a revolt over its demerger plans from shareholders incensed at the firm's determination to install Sir Neville Sims in the joint role of chairman and chief executive and give senior executives potentially unlimited bonus packages. Tarmac's determination to breach conventional corporate governance standards and deprive shareholders of the chance to vote on some of the most controversial aspects of boardroom remuneration have angered senior investors.

Clerical Medical, known for its robust stance on corporate governance issues, has told Tarmac's chairman, Sir John Banham, that it will vote against the whole demerger plan at the extraordinary meeting next Thursday. William Claxton-Smith, Clerical Medical's director of UK equities, said: "It is our view that investors should be given the opportunity to vote separately on substantive and potentially controversial issues ... but the single resolution only allows us to express our opposition by voting against the totality of the demerger. Despite our commercial support for this, we will be doing so."

Other large shareholders... have protested about the company's determination to install Sir Neville in the dual boardroom role. The appointment of a senior non-executive director and the promise of another have gone only part of the way to offset their concerns.

The Association of British Insurers is also seeking clarification of the reward packages which appear to offer unlimited riches to directors of Carillion, the aggregates company being spun out of the group. The ABI wants Tarmac to provide details of the ceiling on incentive packages as well as more information about the performance criteria which will underpin the award of share options and bonuses.

Extract from 'Tarmac investors threaten revolt', *The Guardian,* 02 July 1999

Board members' motivation for resisting or recommending takeovers to their shareholders may stretch trust to the limit. The formal wording always talks dispassionately about the decision being in the best interests of the shareholders. This is inevitable, not least because of how directors perceive their legal duties and obligations. But privately one knows that directors' resistance to takeover bids is influenced by their personal interest in hanging onto their jobs. Once the price has been satisfactorily bid up and their own generous financial parachutes negotiated, they may then 'switch horses' and recommend the takeover.

Think twice about emails

There was a time when the interpersonal components of shadow-side dealings were hidden in private face-to-face meetings and unrecorded telephone calls. Nowadays, when a scandal occurs with accusations of major wrongdoing by senior officers in a company, the shadow side may surface later in embarrassing emails stored on a server, hard drive or back-up tape.

Even if you resort to the telephone, the person called may be too busy to take your call and you'll leave the evidence on their voicemail.

The mistake is to think that emails (and to a lesser extent phone calls) are private. Jo Moore, the spin doctor to the deposed transport secretary Stephen Byers, was undone by her infamous email suggesting that 11 September was a good day to bury some bad news.

Before the days of email, Richard Nixon's conversations were tape-recorded for posterity. While a reasonably successful American president in many ways, and unusually liberal by Republican standards, his tapes revealed him as a vicious, intolerant lunatic, given to long, rambling diatribes about Jews and blacks. With this in mind, a journalist writing in *Sunday Business* offers this advice:

> *Cut and paste a picture of Richard Nixon onto the corner of your email box. As you are tapping out that exhortation to kill and destroy the competition/stitch up the client/bribe the regulator/do something rude with the receptionist, glance up at the great man's smiling face. Then get up and deliver the thought in person. That way you can be sure it will be safely forgotten by lunchtime.*
>
> (Matthew Lynn: 'How e (for excruciating) mail has become a threat to business', *Sunday Business,* 17-18 January 2002)

What is discussible?

After giving his director some highly sensitive information, a manager was surprised by the director's response: "It may be better that I don't know this. If you tell me, then I shall have to know it. Do you want to rethink this and make sure whether you really want me to know this?".

Denial can be taken a stage further. In one company a vice-president of human resources met a consultant off site. He wanted a meeting that would be completely off the record. He then shared his serious concerns about the integrity of the chief executive. He wanted a sounding board. At the end of the meeting he reiterated its off-the-record nature:

> *"We never had this meeting and we did not talk about these issues. If you ever mention it, I will deny it and you will never do any more work for this company or its subsidiaries". In his mind not only was this issue not discussible, but its discussibility was undiscussible.*
>
> (Gerry Egan: 'The shadow side', *Management Today,* September 1993)

A sign of a healthy, open and confident organisation is that there are few undiscussibles and few unmentionables. Unmentionables are so sensitive or taboo that even their undiscussibility cannot be discussed. A valuable role may be performed by an adept HR director in rendering the undiscussibles and unmentionables discussible.

THEME 2 QUESTIONNAIRE: TRUST AND RELATIONSHIPS

ASSESSMENT

Write in empty boxes, complete statements, circle options, or tick where applicable. Numbers equate to points scored.

In your organisation

2.1

In your view, how much is senior management trusted by your employees?				
Don't know	0. Not at all	1. A little	2. Fairly	3. Very
What are they trusted to do?				
What are they not trusted to do?				

2.2

How much is your workforce trusted by your senior managers?				
Don't know	0. Not at all	1. A little	2. Fairly	3. Very
What are they trusted to do?				
What are they not trusted to do?				

2.3

How much do investors trust the senior managers to act in their interest?				
Don't know	0. Not at all	1. A little	2. Fairly	3. Very
What are they trusted to do?				
What are they not trusted to do?				

2.4

How much does the local community trust senior managers to act in their interest?				
Don't know	0. Not at all	1. A little	2. Fairly	3. Very
What are they trusted to do?				
What are they not trusted to do?				

2.5

How much do pressure groups, media and non-governmental organisations (acting on behalf of wider society and future generations) trust the managers to act in their interest?				
Don't know	0. Not at all	1. A little	2. Fairly	3. Very
What are they trusted to do?				
What are they not trusted to do?				

2.6

How much awareness is there that trust is an important issue that may affect business reputation?				
Don't know	0. None	1. A little	2. Some	3. Considerable

2.7

How much effort is spent explicitly by senior managers on trust-related matters?				
Don't know	0. None	1. A little	2. Some	3. Considerable

2.8

To what extent is trust addressed in company policy documents?				
Don't know	0. None	1. A little	2. Some	3. Considerable

2.9

What awareness is there of the risks of potentially damaging recorded messages (email/voicemail)?				
Don't know	0. None	1. A little	2. Some	3. Considerable

2.10

How widespread is the problem of issues not being discussed?				
Don't know	3. Not at all	2. A little	1. Fairly	0. Very

2.11

How widespread is the problem of issues not being able to be mentioned as warranting discussing?				
Don't know	3. Not at all	2. A little	1. Fairly	0. Very

2.12

How extensive is the range of taboo subjects that are undiscussible or unmentionable?				
Don't know	3. Not at all	2. A little	1. Fairly	0. Very

SCORING

Total number of points scored	[ ]	
Out of a possible maximum of	36	
Percentage =	[ ]	%

THEME 2: TRUST AND RELATIONSHIPS

REFLECTIONS

Capture your observations, thoughts and ideas here.

Good ideas that I have picked up:

Important things that my organisation should do:

Urgent things that my organisation should do:

Things that I can and should do myself:

Things that I need to investigate further:

Things that I need to discuss with other people (say whom):

THEME 3: TRAINING AND DEVELOPMENT

Training and development programmes provide a rich seam to mine for shadowside hunters. The reason? Each party to the process needs to feel safe – learners, trainers and developers, and their management sponsors. All want their dignity to be maintained and their security and position protected.

Psychological safety

The need for psychological safety is universal. This is true at all levels in the organisation. Directors are sometimes unwilling to be trained alongside their managers because it would undermine their elevated mystique of being a director. At least they see it this way. Some claim that:

> *They need to be able to respect us. They won't do so if we admit that we need to learn too. When you become a director, people assume you know it all. We have to live up to that.*

At lower levels learners need to feel confident about experimenting with new behaviours. A popular training strategy is to make the experience far removed from daily reality. In one example learners build structures using Lego bricks "to create metaphors and stories that add meaning to our identity, imbuing our descriptions of our workplace with emotion" (according to one training psychologist). However, the cost to the organisation of such 'safe' approaches is high, as learners struggle to find relevance to their work and a way of transferring learning to their job.

Don't learn too much!

Learners may want their trainers to help them challenge their dysfunctional jobs, their bosses and the existing power structure. Managers want their staff to learn, but not so well that they get ideas above their station, become discontent, or want to change their job. Developers want to 'fire up' the learners, but not so much they have unrealistic expectations of what can be accomplished once back at base.

Motives and motivation

On their return from training, learners may find that their new-found skills, ideas and enthusiasm are not as welcome as they had hoped and expected. "You can forget about all that for a start" is not uncommon. Unaligned motives of the learners, sponsors and trainers lead to different and unmet expectations. Trainers categorise attendees into three groups:

- **Learners,** who are genuinely interested in the subject and learning, and are prepared to work and contribute.
- **Holiday-makers,** who regard going on a course as a form of vacation and consequently as a way of getting out of work and relaxing. If they learn, it's a bonus.
- **Prisoners,** who have been sent on the course by their managers, and who generally think they have nothing to learn and that it is a waste of their time.

Who is the developer's client?

Developers can find themselves walking a tightrope, unclear about their respective allegiances and obligations to their 'students' while holding membership of the organisation's management team and having to satisfy the needs and concerns of sponsors. They risk being accused of colluding with their 'students' in subverting what they collectively perceive as dysfunctional behaviour and control processes in the organisation. Yet, if they fail to challenge the status quo and the current power base, they may insufficiently help the organisation sustain itself at a higher level.

> *...directors of courses find themselves in the midst of conflict... when, on the one hand, they assert a traditional professional dedication to the development of each student, but, on the other hand, reassure sponsors that their delegates will make continuing contributions to the corporation. In effect, such reassurances indicate that there will be no change in the dominant dependent relationship.*
>
> (Jonathan Gosling and David Ashton, 'Action Learning and Academic Qualifications', *Management Learning,* Vol. 25 (1994), No. 2)

Simulating real life

In August 2002 the US military conducted the biggest war game in history, with 13,000 troops, at a cost of £165m. But it was rigged to ensure that the Americans beat their 'Middle Eastern' adversaries, according to General Paul Van Riper, a retired marine lieutenant-general.

'MILLENNIUM CHALLENGE' WAR GAME

When General Van Riper agreed to command the forces of an unnamed Middle Eastern state – which bore a strong resemblance to Iraq – he thought he would be given a free rein to probe US weaknesses. But when the game began, he was told to deploy his forces to make life easier for US forces.

"We were directed ... to move air defences so that the army and marine units could successfully land," he said. "We were simply directed to turn [air defence systems] off or move them ... So it was scripted to be whatever the control group wanted it to be."

As the US fleet entered the Gulf, Van Riper gave a signal – not in a radio transmission that might have been intercepted, but in a coded message broadcast from the minarets of mosques at the call to prayer. He sent orders with motorcycle couriers to evade sophisticated electronic eavesdropping equipment. When the US fleet sailed into the Gulf, he instructed his small boats and planes to move around in apparently aimless circles before launching a surprise attack which sank a substantial part of the US navy, including its only aircraft carrier. The war game had to be stopped and the American ships 'refloated' so that the US forces stood a chance.

The war game was advertised as a free-play, in which there are two sides trying to win. The purpose was to validate new 'transformation' concepts that the US armed forces were trying to test "to see if they were robust enough to put into doctrine". But once the US forces started to lose, it simply became a scripted exercise, Van Riper claimed. He found that his orders to his own officers were being overruled by the military commanders of the game.

"Nothing was learned from this," Van Riper said. "A culture not willing to think hard and test itself does not augur well for the future."

Extracts from 'War game was fixed to ensure American victory', *The Guardian,* 21 August, and 'Wake-up call', *The Guardian,* 06 September 2002

You can play these games in two ways: either free-play and unpredictable or prescripted. The problem arises when you confuse the two and want to change the rules mid-game because you are losing.

Playing with fire

Company training departments also play games with learners – often inadvertently – and these similarly can go wrong. One such example occurred in British Bakeries.

BRITISH BAKERIES

British Bakeries used to train its heads of departments in the skills of developing strategies for their own functional areas. Learning as a team under the expert guidance of business educators, they had to produce a radical business strategy for the whole company. They were then required to present their new business strategy to their board of directors. The learning was a rich experience for the managers and the resulting strategy was of high quality. Having worked on their strategy on and off for several months, the managers became very attached to their strategy and considered it superior to their board's. They were then shocked when the board politely listened but then did nothing with their strategy, correctly reminding the 'learners' that it was no more than a learning exercise; that was the deal they had struck with the developers.

Extract from William Tate: 'Linking development with business', in *Leadership in Organizations: Current Issues and Key Trends,* (ed. John Storey), Routledge 2003

The problem arose because the chosen material could have been for real, and the learners desperately wanted it to be. But think about it. How could the board directors have been expected to admit openly that their subordinates' business strategy was superior to their own, whatever its intrinsic merits? That would have called into question the value of the directors' function and their competence. In hindsight the contract between the parties was naïvely flawed and poorly communicated, thereby dangerously raising the learners' expectations.

When considering how to enter into a clear contract with learners and their sponsors, the options facing developers in choosing a learning experience are shown on the continuum set out below.

FIGURE 2
FALSE-REAL LEARNING MATERIAL CONTINUUM

1 VISIBLY FALSE	2 OSTENSIBLY REALISTIC	3 POTENTIALLY REAL	4 LIVE REALITY
Patently removed from real work life (e.g. outdoor pursuits, and games such as how to survive on the moon)	Resembles typical work-type material, but not actually the learner's own or his/ her company's	Genuine learner's company material, but agreed for use only as learning opportunity	The learners' own work problems and needs in context from which to learn and take action

Extract from William Tate: *Developing Corporate Competence,* Gower, 1995

Scapegoating training

Training is frequently invoked for reasons of reputation. The mis-selling of pensions in the UK and elsewhere in the 1990s was an example. This industry-wide scandal represented a collective failure of leadership to address competitive and ethical issues. Yet, for political reasons, company leaders blamed their employees and poor training ('the training wasn't good enough'), and they then launched wholesale retraining in the hope of reassuring customers and winning round public opinion ('Don't worry, we have redesigned the training').

Training is a quick, easy and visible reaction by managers who need to be seen to be doing something. It is far easier than questioning the values and culture of the institution. But training is no substitute for tackling organisational shortcomings.

The real problems usually lie with collective *management* performance (not individual *managerial* performance). They are not to be found on the surface of individual managers' skills, but deep in the organisation's psyche. Training and retraining individuals conveniently points the finger elsewhere.

NOT ME, GOVERNOR

A much-criticised and publicly embattled chief executive, who later lost his job, claimed that he was "surrounded by idiots". He ordered the HR department to run courses in leadership (for others).

While recourse to training may be genuinely well-intentioned and naively expected to deliver a solution, it may be a political ploy.

A lesson in competence

Competency methodology is popular with many large organisations. It forms the basis of the UK Government's system of National Vocational Qualifications (NVQs). NVQs were seen as an important development in the professionalising of the Prison Service and prison officers in particular (see case study at the end of this Audit). Such initiatives can be admirable; competencies may well make a useful contribution. But there are dangers.

The competency approach begins by breaking down a national occupation into its competencies. These apply to individual job-holders. They set down what the elements of tasks in the job look like when they are being performed by an individual correctly. Thus they can form the basis of training. At the end of their training the job-holders may be rewarded with a qualification.

It is important not to confuse the development of individuals in their ongoing current roles with the remedying of institutional shortcomings, the need for organisational change and for change-management skills. Research demonstrates that individualbased initiatives do not hold the solution to complex organisational problems.

The fact that someone has demonstrated that he has the ability to display the required competencies as an individual is no guarantee that the management mix will work as rationally as this in the everyday cut and thrust of prison life. There are several reasons for this:

- **Inter-personal dynamics -** In the prison service case study given later, this is the dynamic between officers, and between officers and prisoners. This exchange may include trading favours or wanting to settle for 'a quiet life'.
- **Choices -** We all exercise choices in our jobs as to what we choose to spend our time on.
- **Missing qualities -** Lists of competencies have difficulty capturing highly personal and variable qualities such as courage, fair-mindedness and energy.

- **Consciousness -** This is what goes on in someone's head. It is not the same as what goes on in their hands ('behaviour'). Competence is concerned with the latter – what they do, not why they choose to do it, or choose not to.

A good example of the problem of consciousness comes from the world of skiing instruction.

APRES SKI

In competency terms, the 'task' of skiing can be analysed and broken down into its various component parts. These can then be taught. The ski instructor might be telling a standing line of beginners to lift one ski off the ground in order to practise 'unweighting'. The instructor assumes that each learner is listening, concentrating and attempting to do as told. But let's imagine what may be going on in their heads. One is scared stiff of falling. Another is looking round for admirers of his latest fashion skiwear. A third is fantasising about the après ski with the handsome Australian instructor.

As this example shows, a definition of competence, and even instruction in that competence, is only part of the rich mix that combines to make performance in practice. While lists of competencies are rational, their practice in reality is corrupted by the human foibles and frailties that dwell in the shadow side.

THEME 3 QUESTIONNAIRE: IS LEARNING GROUNDED IN REALITY?

ASSESSMENT

Write in empty boxes, complete statements, circle options, or tick where applicable. Numbers equate to points scored.

NB: For reasons of simplicity the word 'developers' is used below to cover a range of roles and job titles used by people involved in assisting learning. These include trainers, educators, instructors, lecturers, facilitators and developers.

In your organisation

3.1 How significant is the problem of learners being actively discouraged from implementing what they have learnt?

Don't know | 3. Not at all | 2. A little | 1. Fairly | 0. Very

3.2 How significant is the problem of people on courses being 'holiday makers'?

Don't know | 3. Not at all | 2. A little | 1. Fairly | 0. Very

3.3 How significant is the problem of people being sent on courses against their will as 'prisoners'?

Don't know | 3. Not at all | 2. A little | 1. Fairly | 0. Very

3.4 What use is made of learning methods and materials that are divorced from the reality of your organisation?

Don't know | 3. Not at all | 2. A little | 1. Fairly | 0. Very

3.5 Have your developers ever felt under management pressure to compromise their integrity?

Don't know | 3. Not at all | 2. A little | 1. Fairly | 0. Very

3.6 How torn do your developers feel in their duties to learners and to management sponsors?

Don't know | 3. Not at all | 2. A little | 1. Fairly | 0. Very

3.7 How unreasonably constrained are your developers in what, who and how they conduct their activities?

Don't know | 3. Not at all | 2. A little | 1. Fairly | 0. Very

3.8 How much are your developers encouraged to get close to the business?

Don't know | 0. Not at all | 1. A little | 2. Fairly | 3. Very

3.9 How good is the quality of dialogue between your developers and business leaders?

Don't know | 0. Not at all | 1. A little | 2. Fairly | 3. Very

3.10 Do your developers feel unclear about who sets their agenda?

Don't know | 3. Not at all | 2. A little | 1. Fairly | 0. Very

3.11 Do your developers feel uneasy about who sets their agenda?

Don't know | 3. Not at all | 2. A little | 1. Fairly | 0. Very

3.12	How much do your developers make use of learning contracts to try to avoid later misunderstanding?				
	Don't know	0. Not at all	1. A little	2. Fairly	3. Very
3.13	How much do your developers fear that learning contracts would constrain their freedom?				
	Don't know	0. Not at all	1. A little	2. Fairly	3. Very
3.14	How often is training and development unfairly blamed ('scapegoated') for major organisation performance shortcomings?				
	Don't know	3. Not at all	2. Occasionally	1. Fairly	0. Frequently
	Give examples:				
3.15	How often is training and development unreasonably heralded as the answer to major organisation performance shortcomings?				
	Don't know	3. Not at all	2. Occasionally	1. Fairly	0. Frequently
	Give examples:				
3.16	How big a gap exists between the fine words spoken about the importance of training and development and the reality of the company's commitment?				
	Don't know	3. Not at all	2. A little	1. Fairly	0. Very Large

SCORING

Total number of points scored	☐
Out of a possible maximum of	48
Percentage =	☐ %

THEME 3: TRAINING AND DEVELOPMENT

REFLECTIONS

Capture your observations, thoughts and ideas here.

Good ideas that I have picked up:

Important things that my organisation should do:

Urgent things that my organisation should do:

Things that I can and should do myself:

Things that I need to investigate further:

Things that I need to discuss with other people (say whom):

THEME 4: CREATIVITY AND INNOVATION

There are good and bad ideas. Some ideas need stamping on quickly. But many good ideas are killed off for bad reasons. For example, critics may be envious or feel threatened by change. The shadow side is highly active in the world of ideas. It has much to answer for, but also much to be thanked for.

Look 'outside the box'

People typically try to improve the organisation's workings by tinkering with the rational factors. But these formal aspects of an organisation are relatively weak at bringing about change and innovation.

LIFTING MORALE

On arrival for work in the morning, employees would gather outside the lift doors in their 'skyscraper' office block waiting for the lift to arrive. It was slow and had a long way to descend. People were always complaining. Once in, they complained about the long, slow journey to their floor. The morale problem was so serious that the company spent a fortune on lift engineers trying to speed up the service. All failed. Then one hit on a novel, low-cost solution. He installed mirrors on all the walls. Now the employees were no longer uncomfortable and bored; they could admire and groom themselves while waiting. All complaints ceased.

Things are not always what they seem. If mirrors can speed up lifts, what can photocopiers be used for? Not merely making multiple copies of documents. They are networking venues. They are where you find out what is going on. They provide serendipitous opportunities for chance encounters. Copiers should be located where you want people from different departments to bump into each other.

Skunk works

Organisations, as much as colleagues, can frustrate the development of ideas. A bureaucratic culture's systems, rules and procedures can stifle creativity and innovation. This has led some large companies to house 'skunk works' where the normal rules don't apply.

SKUNK WORKS

The US aeronautical company Lockheed (now Lockheed Martin) originated the skunk works concept in 1943. The term attained generic usage in the 1960s. It means a semiofficial project team that is tacitly licensed to bend the rules and think outside the box. 'Experts' drop out of the mainstream of a company's operations in order to develop some experimental technology or new application in secrecy and at speed, unhampered by bureaucracy or the strict application of regulations.

Leaders of skunk works require a great deal of faith from corporate executives, who generally have no idea what is going on in there.

Ford is one of many companies, in a variety of industries, that now employ the technique.

Extract from William Tate: *The Business Innovation Audit,* Cambridge Strategy Publications, 2003

In setting up a skunk works, a rational solution is recognising non-rational behaviour and legitimising a sub-culture outside the mainstream official structure. It's a bit like the king licensing the court jester to be able to safely say things that are banned for everyone else under the official cultural norms and protocol.

Social and human capital

"It's not what you know; it's who you know." How often we hear this said, sometimes with an air of exasperation. Surely, it's what you know that should really matter and justify personal success in one's job (i.e. rational and fair). 'Who you know' sounds like cheating – using connections and working the system to your own advantage (i.e. non-rational and political).

'What you know' is part of what is nowadays called *human capital* – what is locked up in people's heads. 'Who you know' is part of *social capital* – the value of relationships to an organisation. These words are fast entering the management lexicon.

TAKEOVER LOSSES

A large computer manufacturer took over a niche telecommunications company with a renowned reputation for certain products and components. The buyer wanted to acquire the company's expertise but not its employees and costs. The HR Director was told that she would be well rewarded if she would help make the staff redundant quickly and with the statutory minimum compensation, in spite of the company's more generous usual terms. She resisted, but many were made redundant nonetheless. Others left voluntarily because of the bad climate that this provoked. Collectively, they took with them the technical knowhow in their heads, and the acquiring company was unable to capitalise on its acquisition.

Social capital is the vehicle for safeguarding, releasing, transmitting and applying the tacit knowledge held by individuals. Trusting and open relationships enable sharing to take place. Any organisation that succeeds in combining human capital and social capital stands a good chance of being highly innovative.

Manage the gaps

The implication of the above is the value of focusing attention on the relationships and gaps – between individuals, between departmental functions, and between stakeholders - rather than on the individuals themselves. This is true for managing ideas as well as for performance in general.

For example, organisation consultants seeking business with an organisation shouldn't just think of key individuals as the target for their intervention. Instead they should concentrate on the gaps between key players. This is where their main value-adding ability may well lie. Here are some tips:

- *Pick a team that communicates among its members, rather than one that is a collection of individually superior players.*
- *Reward people for directly sharing their know-how, for including others in their knowledge-sharing networks.*
- *When you transfer employees, watch out for what is happening with their connections.*

(Valdis Krebs: *Working in the Connected World – Managing Connected Assets,* www.orgnet.com)

Not invented here

When confronted with an idea, most people cannot stop themselves from instinctively reacting with reasons against the idea ("it would cost too much", etc). There is the well-known 'not-invented-here' syndrome.

[For a fuller discussion on this subject and how to combat it, see *The Business Innovation Audit* by William Tate, Cambridge Strategy Publications 2003.]

License chaos

At times of change, you can intervene directly in the shadow system to change the balance between the legitimate system and the shadow system. You might need to do this to make the system more chaotic.

NORM BUSTERS

When a new Director of Human Resources joined British Airways in 1984, he quickly made it known that his role was that of 'norm buster'. He wanted department staff to think of themselves as norm busters too. His diagnosis was that the organisation was too traditional, controlled and regulated. There was too much uniformity and adherence to rules, and too little discretion and personal judgement.

THEME 4 QUESTIONNAIRE: ARE YOU HELPING OR HINDERING CREATIVITY AND DIALOGUE?

ASSESSMENT

Write in empty boxes, complete statements, circle options, or tick where applicable. Numbers equate to points scored. In some of the questions the scores 0 – 3 are reversed.

In your organisation

4.1 How common is the not-invented-here syndrome?

Don't know | 3. Not at all | 2. A little | 1. Fairly | 0. Very

4.2 How common is it to find managers taking the credit for others' ideas?

Don't know | 3. Not at all | 2. A little | 1. Fairly | 0. Very

4.3 How common is it to find managers promoting the work reputation of more talented subordinates?

Don't know | 0. Not at all | 1. A little | 2. Fairly | 3. Very

4.4 How well does the informality of office layout encourage the exchange of information and ideas?

Don't know | 0. Not at all | 1. A little | 2. Fairly | 3. Very

4.5 How much is easy access to the internet used to encourage the exchange of information and ideas?

Don't know | 0. Not at all | 1. A little | 2. Fairly | 3. Very

4.6 How accepted is the notion that networking is a positive activity?

Don't know | 0. Not at all | 1. A little | 2. Fairly | 3. Very

4.7 How strongly is networking actively encouraged?

Don't know | 0. Not at all | 1. A little | 2. Fairly | 3. Very

4.8 How much do competency frameworks emphasise the importance of relationships?

Don't know | 0. Not at all | 1. A little | 2. Fairly | 3. Very

4.9 How well is the sharing of know-how recognised and rewarded?

Don't know | 0. Not at all | 1. A little | 2. Fairly | 3. Very

4.10 How much interest is shown in securing people's contacts/connections when they leave or transfer?

Don't know | 0. None | 1. A little | 2. Some | 3. Considerable

4.11 How much interest is shown in key employees' tacit know-how at times of reorganisation?

Don't know | 0. None | 1. A little | 2. Some | 3. Considerable

4.12 In using successful teams, how strong is the focus on the gaps between members?

Don't know | 0. Not at all | 1. A little | 2. Fairly | 3. Very

4.13 How much awareness is there of the idea of 'norm busters'?

Don't know | 0. None | 1. A little | 2. Some | 3. Considerable

4.14 How much are norm busters needed at present?

Don't know | 0. Not at all | 1. A little | 2. Fairly | 3. Very

4.15 How much are norm busters made welcome?

Don't know | 0. Not at all | 1. A little | 2. Fairly | 3. Very

You personally

4.16 How common is the not-invented-here syndrome in your own response to ideas from other departments?

Don't know | 3. Not at all | 2. A little | 1. Fairly | 0. Very

4.17 How common is the not-invented-here syndrome in your own response to ideas from subordinates?

Don't know | 3. Not at all | 2. A little | 1. Fairly | 0. Very

4.18 How strongly do you promote the work reputation of more talented subordinates?

Don't know | 0. Not at all | 1. A little | 2. Fairly | 3. Very

4.19 How aware are you of how informal office arrangements encourage the exchange of information and ideas?

Don't know | 0. Not at all | 1. A little | 2. Fairly | 3. Very

4.20 How much do you use informal office arrangements to encourage the exchange of information and ideas?

Don't know | 0. None | 1. A little | 2. Some | 3. Considerable

4.21 How easy do you make people's access to the internet to encourage the exchange of information and ideas?

Don't know | 0. Not at all | 1. A little | 2. Fairly | 3. Very

4.22 How strongly do you accept the notion that networking is a positive activity?

Don't know | 0. Not at all | 1. A little | 2. Fairly | 3. Very

4.23 How strongly do you encourage networking?

Don't know | 0. Not at all | 1. A little | 2. Fairly | 3. Very

4.24 How willingly do you accept that 'who you know' has legitimacy as well as 'what you know'?

Don't know | 0. Not at all | 1. A little | 2. Fairly | 3. Very

4.25 How much value do you place on the importance of relationships to innovation?

Don't know | 0. None | 1. A little | 2. Some | 3. Considerable

SCORING

Your organisation			**Yourself**		
Total number of points scored	☐		Total number of points scored	☐	
Out of a possible maximum of	45		Out of a possible maximum of	30	
Percentage =	☐	%	Percentage =	☐	%

Total number of points scored	☐	
Out of a possible maximum of	75	
Percentage =	☐	%

Where the same question is repeated, first for your organisation and then for yourself, you may wish to check whether you personally are ahead of or behind the organisation generally.

THEME 4: CREATIVITY AND INNOVATION

REFLECTIONS

Capture your observations, thoughts and ideas here.

Good ideas that I have picked up:

Important things that my organisation should do:

Urgent things that my organisation should do:

Things that I can and should do myself:

Things that I need to investigate further:

Things that I need to discuss with other people (say whom):

THEME 5:
REWARD AND PUNISHMENT

'Do this and you'll get that' – whether as a reward or a punishment – is a widely used manipulative strategy for raising children, teaching students and managing workers. But such devices imply and engender mistrust. Even announcing incentives can cause offence. Managers who use rewards and punishment to get what they want are taking risks with the messy shadow side of human behaviour.

A personal need to control

Managing people, by definition, means exercising external control. Rewards and punishment are the ultimate manifestation of external controls. Some people say that management's use of reward and punishment has its roots in Newtonian physics, where every force has a reaction. According to this theory, movement is assumed not possible until an external force acts upon it (though a new theory of 'Perception Control' is now challenging that idea as far as human behaviour is concerned).

The Theory X side of the concept famously espoused by Douglas McGregor is another piece of the jigsaw.

Theory X

1. The average human being has an inherent dislike of work and will avoid it if he can.
2. Because of this human characteristic of dislike of work, most people must be coerced, controlled, directed, threatened with punishment to get them to put forth adequate effort toward the achievement of organisational objectives.
3. The average human being prefers to be directed, wishes to avoid responsibility, has relatively little ambition, wants security above all.

Theory Y

1. The expenditure of physical and mental effort at work is as natural as play or rest.
2. External control and the threat of punishment are not the only means for bringing about effort toward organisational objectives. Man will exercise self-direction and self-control in the service of objectives to which he is committed.
3. Commitment to objectives is a function of the rewards associated with their achievement. (The most significant of such rewards; e.g. the satisfaction of ego and self-actualisation needs, can be direct products of effort directed toward organisational objectives.)
4. The average human being learns, under proper conditions, not only to accept but to seek responsibility.
5. The capacity to exercise a relatively high degree of imagination, ingenuity, and creativity in the solution of organisational problems is widely, not narrowly, distributed in the population.

1. Under the conditions of modern industrial life, the intellectual potentialities of the average human being are only partially utilized.

Douglas McGregor: *The Human Side of Enterprise,* McGraw-Hill, 1960

There is a burgeoning industry in incentive and bonus packages that assumes individuals cannot be relied upon to do the right things, or apply sufficient effort, without monetary carrots (beyond salary) being dangled in front of their noses.

Even training – generally more rooted in Theory Y beliefs – is experimenting with the idea that financial incentives are increasingly needed to tempt people into accepting training.

People like James Dyson, the vacuum machine manufacturer, appear to be increasingly in the minority and swimming against the tide:

> *Anyone who needs a bonus to motivate them is not the right person to be working here.*

But if employees' interests are aligned with those of the business in a 'high commitment' organisation, there should be no need for incentives.

Mixed messages

Organisations seem increasingly keen that their managers adopt a facilitative or coaching style (Theory Y) in place of traditional command and control (Theory X). The UK's National Heath Service is pushing this message hard. It practice, managers find it very difficult to make this kind of change, for these reasons:

Habits
The managers have familiar patterns of behaviour that they are confident about.

Role expectations
They have expectations of what it means to be a manager. What's the point of being a manager if one isn't in charge?

Accountability
They wonder how they can be held accountable if they are not in charge.

Structure
The conventional organisation chart reinforces formal lines of reporting and accountability for which managers are rewarded. This sends a message that reinforces Theory X.

Followers
Other people have expectations of how they relate to a manager. How empowered do followers want to be? (One can imagine a dialogue: "You decide". "No, you decide.")

Daily pressures
In the hurly-burly pressures of the moment, Theory X takes over, despite our best intentions. Most us have heard others (or ourselves) say in exasperation: "Just do it!".

The bitten bite back

Managers who firmly believe in Theory X for their staff (though they may think of themselves as Theory Y!) incline towards rewards and punishment as legitimate weapons in the armoury of tools available to get the organisation's needs met. But as Marshall Rosenberg points out:

> *I learned that I could make all the demands in the world but still couldn't make the children do anything. This is a humbling lesson in power for those of us who believe that, because we're a parent, teacher, or manager, our job is to change other people and make them behave. Here were these youngsters letting me know that I couldn't make them do anything. All I could do was make them wish they had – through punishment. Then eventually they taught me that any time I was foolish enough to make them wish they had complied by punishing them, they had ways of making me wish that I hadn't!*
>
> (Marshall B Rosenberg: *Nonviolent Communication,* Puddle Dancer Press, 1999)

Rosenberg asks himself two questions when he wants someone to do something different:

> *"What do I want this person to do that's different from what he or she is currently doing?"*

The second question rarely gets considered:

> *"What do I want this person's reasons to be for doing what I'm asking?"*

It is the answer to this second question that shows why punishment is unlikely to work. Punishment and reward interfere with people's ability to do things motivated by the reasons we'd like them to have. If a manager's requirement is put in such a way that the person has only two possible responses – submit or rebel – neither outcome is satisfactory.

Two sides of the same coin

Punishment and rewards appear to be opposite sides of the same coin. But the view is growing that there is very little that differentiates them. Indeed, in one school of thought, incentives are themselves a form of punishment:

> *... while manipulating people with incentives seems to work in the short run, it is a strategy that ultimately fails and even does lasting harm. ... people actually do inferior work when they are enticed with money, grades or other incentives. The more we use artificial inducements to motivate people, the more they lose interest in what we're bribing them to do. ... Even praise can become a verbal bribe.*
>
> (Alfie Kohn, *Punished by Rewards,* Houghton Mifflin, 1993)

While the subtle relationship between punishment and rewards needs understanding, so does that between straightforward 'thank-you' *rewards* after the event, and 'if-you-perform' *incentives* (and the implied 'if-you-don't') before the event.

Incentives are more manipulative than 'thank-you' rewards. But the distinction between the two blurs once payments become repetitive and expected. The language is frequently loose too: rewards may be spoken about as incentives. Both may be referred to as 'bonuses'. That said, thinking about the distinction and what it implies for both parties' motives, can be valuable.

In reality, in spite of their mythical powers, incentives rarely bring much genuine improvement. The head of one of the UK's leading consultancies on executive pay admitted this in an interview. When asked:

> *"Does performance-related pay motivate anybody?"*

He then answered a slightly different question by saying:

> *"I don't think somebody is going to work better or harder at the top level because they have one kind of incentive plan or another."*
>
> ('Nobody's hero', *The Guardian,* 02 August 2003)

Most organisation performance is a product of the system rather than of individuals' effort. The promise of huge bonuses to directors of failing public rail services is unlikely to make the trains run on time. Offering them blatant and substantial incentives to improve the safety record is naïve and offensive.

The quality guru W. Edwards Deming used to point out that it is possible to achieve more by improving the system's weaknesses than by trying to manage individuals' performance and productivity.

While many managers continue to believe that people need incentives to 'motivate' them to do good work, there is also a view that incentives get you less:

Incentives only motivate people to get the incentive, regardless of the impact on their organisation. Worse, incentives debase the task. Psychologists know that if you put two groups to work, give one group an incentive and the other nothing, then call a coffee break – the group with the incentive stops work while the group with no incentive carries on with the task.

(John Seddon, *Vanguard News,* October 2002)

Risks and unintended consequences

Watch out for the distorting effect of incentives and some unintended consequences.

The [bonus] scheme is unlikely to affect the intensity of his effort but it will affect the intensity of his interest in how numbers that report that effort are compiled.

(John Kay, 'Incentive plans that corrode integrity', *Financial Times,* 05 May 2002)

A great deal of individual inventiveness goes into manipulating the reporting of performance in a way that presents it in the most favourable light and thereby earns the bonus. It may lead to individuals claiming credit at others' expense.

DO-IT-YOURSELF BONUSES

A scheme launched in 1996 by B&Q for their store managers badly misfired and attracted bad publicity. The scheme was based on the principle that, in addition to salary, a store manager would receive a percentage of the profit achieved by that store beyond a certain minimum level. There was no upper limit to what could be earned. What happened was that the DIY market picked up unexpectedly and some lucky store managers were due to receive a total payment of several times their salary. So a cap was introduced retrospectively. Result: demotivation all round.

People like money, so it is tempting to think that designing a scheme to give money away is easy. Far from it. Before embarking on such a scheme, it is important for the organisation to think very clearly about:

- the *aims* behind the scheme
- the *assumptions* the company is making
- the potential *risks* to the company

Bonus scheme pitfalls

- The economic forecast may turn out to be wrong.
- The target level to trigger bonus payments may turn out to have been pitched wrongly.

Additionally, the scheme may:

- prove too expensive for the company
- demotivate those outside the scheme
- demotivate the managers themselves
- produce a backlash from shareholders
- damage team effort
- increase turnover of managers or other employees
- lead to malpractices
- lead to managers easing off once the target has been hit
- lead to an exodus of managers immediately following the bonus payout
- encourage short-term behaviour at the expense of the longer term
- detract from a customer-first culture (e.g. cheaper quality goods substituted)
- generate bad publicity

The blindingly obvious

Stupidity is one of Egan's categories of organisational shadow-side behaviour. Bonuses for meeting targets frequently exhibit this quality.

FIRE FIGHTING

Firemen in the New York Fire Service were offered bonuses according to how many fires they put out. There were two problems with this idea. First, the firemen had no influence over their ultimate effectiveness; i.e. whether or not they put out a fire (surprisingly, 100% were put out!). Secondly, they had no influence over their workload; they simply had to respond to other people's fires. Until, that is, they realised that if they started fires they got paid more. Seriously!

Not quite so bizarrely, the chairman of a UK Plc. negotiated a generous so-called incentive plan that paid him a large bonus if he recruited a new chief executive. It was hardly likely that he would fail to achieve this target.

THEME 5 QUESTIONNAIRE: ARE YOUR REWARDS REWARDING OR PUNISHING YOU?

ASSESSMENT

Write in empty boxes, complete statements, circle options, or tick where applicable. Numbers equate to points scored. In some of the questions the scores 0 – 3 are reversed.

5.1 How aware are you of whether you consider other people's attitudes to work are in line with McGregor's Theory X or his Theory Y?

Don't know | 0. Not at all | 1. A little | 2. Fairly | 3. Very

5.2 How aware are you of whether your own attitude to work is in line with McGregor's Theory X or his Theory Y?

Don't know | 0. Not at all | 1. A little | 2. Fairly | 3. Very

5.3 Does the way you manage imply a belief that other people's attitudes to work are more in line with McGregor's Theory X or his Theory Y?

Theory X ☐ Theory Y ☐

5.4 Which of McGregor's theories best sums up the way you are managed?

Theory X ☐ Theory Y ☐

5.5 How strongly would you like to believe other people's attitudes to work are in line with McGregor's Theory Y?

Don't know | 0. Not at all | 1. A little | 2. Fairly | 3. Very

5.6 Which of McGregor's theories would you expect to best sum up other people's attitudes towards their own work (i.e. how they want to be managed)?

Theory X ☐ Theory Y ☐

5.7 Which of McGregor's theories appears to underpin your organisation's culture?

Theory X ☐ Theory Y ☐

5.8 When you need to improve the organisation's performance or resolve its problems, how much do you focus your energy on improving work systems?

Don't know | 0. Not at all | 1. A little | 2. Fairly | 3. Very

5.9 When you need to improve the organisation's performance or resolve its problems, how much do you focus your energy on improving individuals' motivation through the reward system?

Don't know | 3. Not at all | 2. A little | 1. Fairly | 0. Very

5.10

How carefully do you distinguish between making requests and making demands?				
Don't know	0. Not at all	1. A little	2. Fairly	3. Very

5.11

How much use does your organisation make of threats to back up demands?				
Don't know	3. None	2. A little	1. Some	0. Considerable

5.12

How much use do you personally make of threats to back up demands?				
Don't know	3. None	2. A little	1. Some	0. Considerable

5.13

How much use does your organisation make of bribes/incentives to back up demands?				
Don't know	3. None	2. A little	1. Some	0. Considerable

5.14

How much use do you personally make of bribes/incentives to back up demands?				
Don't know	3. None	2. A little	1. Some	0. Considerable

5.15

When you give verbal rewards (e.g. 'well done'), how aware are you of the hierarchical implications?				
Don't know	0. Not at all	1. A little	2. Fairly	3. Very

5.16

When you give such verbal rewards, how frequently would you be trying to shape/manipulate future behaviour?				
Don't know	3. Not at all	2. A little	1. Fairly	0. Very

5.17

If people do what you require of them, how concerned are you with their reasons for doing so?				
Don't know	0. Not at all	1. A little	2. Fairly	3. Very

5.18

How often has an incentive (or hoped-for reward) caused you to do something that you would not otherwise have done? *(No points)*				
Don't know	Not at all	A little	Fairly	Very
Give examples:				

5.19

When you have been on the receiving end of an incentive to deliver against a goal/target, how often have you undertaken an activity to meet the target but which was detrimental to the purpose behind the target? *(No points)*				
Don't know	Not at all	A little	Fairly	Very

5.20

When you have received a reward along with others, how frequently has your emotional response been deferred until you have found out how much others have received? *(No points)*				
Don't know	Not at all	A little	Fairly	Very

5.21

How often have you felt mistrusted or manipulated when on the receiving end of an incentive? *(No points)*				
Don't know	Not at all	A little	Fairly	Very

SCORING

Total number of points scored	☐
Out of a possible maximum of	39
Percentage =	☐ %

THEME 5: REWARD AND PUNISHMENT

REFLECTIONS

Capture your observations, thoughts and ideas here.

Good ideas that I have picked up:

Important things that my organisation should do:

Urgent things that my organisation should do:

Things that I can and should do myself:

Things that I need to investigate further:

Things that I need to discuss with other people (say whom):

THEME 6: TARGET SETTING

Targets straddle the rational/non-rational divide. They share this characteristic with competencies and numbers. Targets appear to be a rational management device for managing desired business results. Used judiciously (thoughtfully, sensitively and minimally) targets can provide direction, priorities and goals. However, there are also numerous problems; among them:

- A lack of identification by those on the receiving end with the target-setter's view of the problem, and thus a lack of ownership of the targets.

- A failure by the target setter to understand the complex reasons for the current, inadequate level of performance. More often than not this has to do with the system's capability, rather than people's efforts, skills or goodwill.

Targets may have their origins in the shadow side. They also frequently promote shadow-side behaviour as a response by those who have targets imposed on them.

Born out of frustration

Targets are used to impose control within hierarchies, or by external authorities – especially government. When frustrated with poor results, slow pace of improvement, and without close executive control or sufficiently detailed managerial knowledge of what needs to be done, or what the system can deliver, top executives (and government ministers) frequently seek recourse to imposing unwelcome and often uninformed targets – on others. As well as setting targets for ends, they may use them in connection with means.

Public sector delivery

The private sector is not immune (see Theme 9 on 'Organisation Culture' for examples in the legal and accountancy professions). But it is in the public sector that the practice is most notorious and the butt of much criticism.

The UK government has elevated the role of targets as its favoured management device for improving the public sector. Since coming to office in 1997 the government has set around 8,000 targets or indicators of success.

In this 'target culture' there is even a centrally set target for increased employee involvement in the NHS; the irony appears lost on the target-setters.

The game has started to unravel and backfire. If the targets are met, the target-setter gets no credit. If they fail, the target-setter is blamed.

Unintended consequences

Targets can be counterproductive. Paradoxically, they can stifle the very behaviour they seek to measure. The National Heath Service in particular provides rich pickings.

BYPASS OPERATIONS

The UK Government's National Audit Office found that, to avoid being fined for over-long waiting lists, 20 per cent of consultants 'frequently ignored clinical priorities in their operations lists, performing simple routine procedures rather than complicated urgent ones in order to make their numbers.

(Simon Caulkin: 'On target for destruction', *The Observer*, 05 August 2001)

If you give people targets and make their careers dependent on delivering them, they will likely meet the targets – even if they have to destroy the enterprise to do it.

The wrong kind of targets can block the mind to what else you could or should be doing, could or should do differently, or what has changed in the system since the target was set.

One of the Department of Health's numerous targets is designed to measure the time patients take to get treatment in casualty. But these don't measure the time they arrive, but the time between being seen and getting treatment. One 88-year old patient waited 24 hours to be treated, but was recorded as having officially been there for only 30 minutes.

SICK TARGETS

When people arrive at hospital Accident & Emergency units, they may be held in the care of the ambulance staff until the hospital is ready to see them. This ploy means that patients have not officially been delivered to the hospital. The consequence is that the clock has not begun to tick. The downside is that the ambulance crew cannot get on with another call, so the official performance of the ambulance service (which is measured separately) is impaired.

The wrong kind of creativity

Targets are a wonderful stimulus to creativity. There's a rule that patients should not be kept on hospital trolleys for more than four hours. Some hospitals have got round this by putting them in chairs. Others have redesignated trolleys as 'mobile beds'. Some hospitals have redesignated corridors as 'rooms' in order to meet a target designed to cut back on the use of corridors to hold patients in trolleys.

System capability

What is the alternative to targets? According to Caulkin:

> *... hard, continuous work to improve the capability of the system from the customer's point of view – [but this] runs counter to politicians' and shareholders' desire for instant fixes.*

An organisation is a system. A system has a capability.

> *If you have a stable system, there is no use to specify a goal. You will get whatever the system will deliver. A goal beyond the capability of the system will not be reached. If you have not got a stable system, there is no point in setting a goal. There is no way to know what the system will produce.*
>
> (W. Edwards Deming, quoted in *The Observer,* 05 August 2001)

Target life-cycle

There is a well-known cycle that operates between centralisation and decentralisation.

> *Both structures have their own weaknesses. Solving one set of organisational problems brings with it the inherent weaknesses contained in its alternative. Eventually, the need for the countervailing set of forces becomes apparent. For example, Pilkington's federal structure meant that it had 27 different specifications for hard hats. With such a proliferation of practices, centralisation becomes the logical way to regain control over standards and costs.*
>
> (William Tate, *Demerging Organisations,* FT Management, 1999)

In line with this principle, centralised target setting will in due course be replaced by local freedom and discretion. Institutions will be allowed to focus on their own priorities for improvement. But, as the Pilkington example shows, there is a price – a proliferation of standards, upsetting for those who value uniformity or are pledged to deliver a single national service.

But there is no happy medium: you have to be centralising or decentralising. So eventually, the wheel will turn again; concern about different standards, coupled with impatience at the centre, will result in a bout of centralised targets again.

THEME 6 QUESTIONNAIRE: ARE YOUR TARGETS ON TARGET?

ASSESSMENT

Write in empty boxes, complete statements, circle options, or tick where applicable. Numbers equate to points scored. In some of the questions the scores 0 – 3 are reversed.

Your organisation

6.1 How much does your organisation currently make use of selective targets to indicate direction, indicate priorities and set goals?

Don't know | 0. Not at all | 1. A little | 2. Fairly | 3. Very

6.2 How much does your organisation currently make use of targets to drive performance and productivity?

Don't know | 3. Not at all | 2. A little | 1. Fairly | 0. Very

6.3 How aware is your organisation of the controversies surrounding the use of targets?

Don't know | 0. Not at all | 1. A little | 2. Fairly | 3. Very

6.4 How concerned is your organisation about the controversies surrounding the use of targets?

Don't know | 0. Not at all | 1. A little | 2. Fairly | 3. Very

6.5 How aware and concerned is your organisation about the following aspects of the use of targets?

Aware and concerned about:	Aware (1 point each)	Concerned about (1 point each)
- who feels ownership of the targets	☐	☐
- who considers their work is being distorted to meet targets	☐	☐
- who is stopping other work to measure and report on targets	☐	☐
- who thinks that your customers are suffering as a result of targets	☐	☐
- who believes they have to behave unethically to meet targets	☐	☐
- who is fiddling their measurement or reporting against targets	☐	☐
- who is suffering considerable stress as a result of targets set for them	☐	☐
- who is changing their priorities against their judgement to meet targets	☐	☐
- who is forced to focus excessively on today's performance rather than tomorrow's	☐	☐

6.6 Is your organisation more interested in the absolute level of performance, or with the amount of improvement? *(No points)*

Absolute level of performance	Amount of improvement	Both in equal measure	Neither	Don't know
☐	☐	☐	☐	☐

6.7 Does your organisation use targets mainly to set absolute levels of performance to be achieved, or to set amounts of improvement to be achieved? *(No points)*

Absolute level of performance	Amount of improvement	Both in equal measure	Neither	Don't know
☐	☐	☐	☐	☐

6.8 How interested is your organisation in results achieved, in comparison with the way those results are achieved? *(No points)*

Actual reults achieved	How results are achieved	Both in equal measure	Neither	Don't know
☐	☐	☐	☐	☐

6.9 How much does your organisation encourage people to set their own targets?

Don't know   0. Not at all   1. A little   2. Fairly   3. Very

6.10 Give examples of targets set by others for your organisation that are:

- unnecessary (your organisation would be doing this anyway)

- ill-conceived (the targets miss the point)

- counter-productive (the targets lead to a bad outcome)

6.11 Where/how would your organisation like to change the way targets are used?

6.12 Where does your organisation have freedom to change the way targets are used?

6.13 What are the main key performance indicators for which targets are or might be valid for your organisation?

You personally

6.14 How much do you personally currently make use of selective targets to indicate direction, indicate priorities and set goals?

Don't know   0. Not at all   1. A little   2. Fairly   3. Very

6.15

How much do you currently make use of targets to drive performance and productivity?				
Don't know	3. Not at all	2. A little	1. Fairly	0. Very

6.16

How aware are you of the controversies surrounding the use of targets?				
Don't know	0. Not at all	1. A little	2. Fairly	3. Very

6.17

How concerned are you about the controversies surrounding the use of targets?				
Don't know	0. Not at all	1. A little	2. Fairly	3. Very

6.18

How aware and concerned are you about the following aspects of the use of targets?

Aware and concerned about:	Aware	Concerned about
	1 point each	
- who feels ownership of the targets	☐	☐
- who considers their work is being distorted to meet targets	☐	☐
- who is stopping other work to measure and report on targets	☐	☐
- who thinks that your customers are suffering as a result of targets	☐	☐
- who believes they have to behave unethically to meet targets	☐	☐
- who is fiddling their measurement or reporting against targets	☐	☐
- who is suffering considerable stress as a result of targets set for them	☐	☐
- who is changing their priorities against their judgement to meet targets	☐	☐
- who is forced to focus excessively on today's performance rather than tomorrow's	☐	☐

6.19

Are you more interested in the absolute level of performance, or with the amount of improvement? *(No points)*

Absolute level of performance	Amount of improvement	Both in equal measure	Neither	Don't know
☐	☐	☐	☐	☐

6.20

Do you use targets mainly to set absolute levels of performance to be achieved, or to set amounts of improvement to be achieved? *(No points)*

Absolute level of performance	Amount of improvement	Both in equal measure	Neither	Don't know
☐	☐	☐	☐	☐

6.21

How interested are you in results achieved, in comparison with the way those results are achieved? *(No points)*

Actual reults achieved	How results are achieved	Both in equal measure	Neither	Don't know
☐	☐	☐	☐	☐

6.22

How much do you encourage people to set their own targets?				
Don't know	0. Not at all	1. A little	2. Fairly	3. Very

6.23 Give examples of targets set by others for your you that are:
- unnecessary (you would be doing this anyway)

- ill-conceived (the targets miss the point)

- counter-productive (the targets lead to a bad outcome)

6.24 Give examples of targets that you set for others that may (on reflection) be:
- unnecessary (they would be doing this anyway)

- ill-conceived (the targets miss the point)

- counter-productive (the targets lead to a bad outcome)

6.25 Where/how would you like to change to change the way targets are used?

6.26 Where do you have freedom to change the way targets are used?

6.27 What are the main key performance indicators for which targets are or might be valid for you?

SCORING

Your organisation			**Yourself**		
Total number of points scored	☐		Total number of points scored	☐	
Out of a possible maximum of	33		Out of a possible maximum of	33	
Percentage =	☐	%	Percentage =	☐	%

Total number of points scored	☐	
Out of a possible maximum of	66	
Percentage =	☐	%

Where the same question is repeated, first for your organisation and then for yourself, you may wish to check whether you personally are ahead of or behind the organisation generally.

THEME 6: TARGET SETTING

REFLECTIONS

Capture your observations, thoughts and ideas here.

Good ideas that I have picked up:

Important things that my organisation should do:

Urgent things that my organisation should do:

Things that I can and should do myself:

Things that I need to investigate further:

Things that I need to discuss with other people (say whom):

THEME 7: MANAGEMENT BY NUMBERS

Every manager knows two things about numbers. One: that there is a 'numbers game' (especially at budget time). Two: that there are 'lies, damned lies and statistics'.

Experience and education makes managers wary of numbers, especially other peoples'. It also makes some managers adept at using numbers for self-serving purposes. Numbers – for all their supposed rationality, objectivity and abstract nature – are equally at home in the darker recesses of the shadow side.

Managers may be proactive in their requirement for numbers (sometimes when they shouldn't be). But managers also find themselves on the receiving end of other officials' requirements to 'deliver the numbers'.

There are two challenges: how to use numbers appropriately, and how to get round them when their use is inappropriate – how to beat the number crunchers at their own game.

Uses and abuses

Numbers are vital in business. They help set targets. They may thereby pressurise others to deliver the results that they want or that they believe the organisation or its stakeholders need.

But numbers have a well-known sinister and suspect quality. Despite their frequent unbelievability, management culture continues to resort to numbers when they shouldn't. Numbers are often elevated as *the* only worthwhile measure of success. If something cannot be measured, then it cannot be important – or so some people assume. Therein lies danger.

There are equal risks in not valuing or attempting to measure what plainly matters but is difficult to measure, as well as measuring (often to excess) what can easily be measured. A good instance of the latter occurs in call centres.

CALL-CENTRE INDUSTRY

'It has a very high burn-out rate, a turnover of staff between 60 and 80% every year and – with a few notable exceptions – it's making the relations between companies and customers even worse than before. And the main reason is that, because of all that IT equipment, every moment of staff time can be measured.

Building customer loyalty is hard to quantify, so what gets measured is how quickly staff can get callers off the phone. That's the bottom line. Even the few seconds between calls – known as 'post-call rap time' – gets measured and logged. And then companies wonder why their customers hate them.

Behind all this measuring is an old-fashioned world view. The idea that large bureaucracies can be managed by numbers. ... everything can be measured and what can be measured can be managed. It simply isn't true.'

David Boyle, *The Tyranny of Numbers,* HarperCollins, 1999

False reports

Numbers are used to provide needed reassurance to a sceptical public or shareholders that things are OK or are getting better. An example occurs when managers are under pressure from investors and want to present better news than is really justified.

INCOME SMOOTHING

Definition: managing balance sheets in such a way that a corporation's profits rise smoothly and predictably (just beating the "forecasts" which investor relations departments have fed to Wall Street analysts) ... One way of smoothing income is to have a "cookie jar", or a reserve of earnings that have not yet been declared on the balance sheet. A good moment to create or replenish a cookie jar is when a corporation takes a "big bath" or reports a large loss ...

Extract from 'A philosophical investigation into Enron', *London Review of Books,* 26 May 2003

Worse than this, in a few extreme cases a whole enterprise may be sustained for a while on an edifice propped up by falsified numbers that have no foundation in reality. Or they may be so arcane or convoluted that no one in a position of supervision can understand them. This may even be true of the auditors, assuming that they are allowed to see them.

NO DEFENCE

The anti-corruption legislation passed by the United States Congress in the wake of the Enron scandal requires chief executive officers to sign a statement to the effect that they endorse their company's figures (to avoid the defence that they didn't know and therefore cannot be held liable if things go wrong). The trouble is that they still may not understand them.

Budgets

The modern-day budget has uses (and abuses) far beyond the original intention of being a means of tracking costs and cash flows. In times of rapid change and increasing competition, in place of flexibility and initiative, the budget becomes an instrument of self-destruction, according to Jeremy Hope and Robin Fraser, co-authors of *Beyond Budgeting* (Harvard Business School Press, 2003). Budgets prevent adaptation, disempower subsidiaries and demoralise staff.

> *In companies the ubiquitous consequence of traditional budgeting is frenzied internal politicking as managers scheme to keep their targets low while ensuring that they spend every penny of their allocation. As Hope says, 'the budget is the protector of cost'.*
>
> (Simon Caulkin, 'An end to the numbers game', *The Observer,* 13 April 2003.)

Measuring the unmeasurable

In a target-driven government culture, NHS staff complain that their work is increasingly driven by what can be measured instead of what matters to their patients.

There is a school of thought that says if something cannot be measured it cannot be valued, managed and improved. But where does that leave a loving marriage? Many of the most important things at work – as in life – cannot be measured.

There is a radical and counter school of thought that claims that managers should not spend their time on anything that can be measured. The argument runs that such things are not those that are most vital to an organisation's future success. Both these schools' extreme positions are untenable.

Measuring intangibles

Measuring things accurately when they lend themselves to measurement is difficult enough. A different challenge – and one that is currently occupying some of the best brains – is how to measure things that cannot be easily measured and reduced to numbers (so-called 'intangibles'). Examples include the value of a company's relationships, its reputation or the quality of its leadership.

In instances such as these there are people – especially in the investment community – who would be glad of numbers as a means of measuring both the current state and as a way of tracking progress.

ACCOUNTING FOR PEOPLE

A task force 'Accounting for People' is asking this question in relation to employees. It aims to put a new range of employee information into companies' annual reports to shareholders that demonstrates the value, rather than the cost, of people.

Tyranny of numbers

David Boyle is a senior associate at the New Economics Foundation. His The Tyranny of Numbers (HarperCollins, 1999) is essential reading for any manager who wants to view the numbers-crazed world through a crystal-clear lens. Boyle offers ten paradoxical ways in which numbers can bite you, a few of which are briefly summarised below:

- **You change what you are counting by counting it.**
  To make trains more punctual, train companies simply lengthen the official journey times.

HALF-SIZE TRAINERS

A training manager was instructed by his boss to halve the length of all the training department's courses in order that twice the number of people would then be able to receive training. Since the company's board received monthly reports on the number of people being trained, this would immediately give the impression that the department's productivity had doubled.

- **The more accurately we count, the more unreliable the figures are.**
  Cost-benefit experts spend enormous efforts getting a figure absolutely correct – only to throw in something else which is simply picked from the air.

KEEPING TRACK OF NUMBERS

In 1844 the French statistician Adolphe Jullien worked out precisely the cost of moving one unit of traffic on their new rail system. He finally came up with a wonderfully exact figure of 0.01254 francs per kilometre. When asked about administration and the interest on capital, he said these were more difficult to assess, so promptly doubled the figure.

- **The more we count, the less we can compare the figures.**
  The figures in the example below were probably honest, but the one thing they failed to provide was objective information. For that you need interpretation, quality and imagination.

ERODING FAITH

A set of 22 studies was carried out to establish the extent of erosion in Sri Lanka. The figures varied by as much as 8,000 fold. The lowest had been collected by a research institute wanting to show how safe their land management was. The highest came from a third world development agency showing how much soil erosion was damaging the environment.

- **Measurements have a monstrous life of their own.**
  Stalin announced his first five-year plan in 1928, an enormous undertaking designed to increase industrial output by 235.9 per cent. The figure was completely spurious, intended to lend a scientific legitimacy to the whole enterprise.

> **BODY COUNT**
>
> **How do you measure the success of a military unit in the Vietnam War? Answer: body count. Result: Terrible loss of life among the Vietnamese, but no American victory.**

- **When you count things, they get worse.**
  Once you start looking at numbers you keep falling over a strange phenomenon. Official statistics tend to get worse when society is worried about something.

> **CHILD ABUSE**
>
> **When unprecedented publicity catapulted the issue of child abuse to the top of the public agenda in 1984, reported incidents shot up by 90%.**

Individuals' performance management

As a service to corporate clients, a large HR consultancy measures managers' competency to two decimal points (e.g. "He has competency gap of 8.32"). Clients take career life and death decisions based on these numbers.

> **IT'S ALL INVENTED**
>
> **In a Middle East airline this spurious rating scheme was used. Out of a possible score of 5, Executive L scored 3.19, and Executive E scored 2.76. The average over eleven executives was 2.80. Executive L's future was safe, but Executive E's was in doubt. Four executives with a score of 2.20 were removed from their jobs.**

Extract from William Tate: *Developing Managerial Competence,* Gower, 1995

Rating scales are popular (with managers) in appraisal schemes. Organisations find it convenient to use a number (or sometimes a letter or word) as a proxy for a highly complex mix of qualitative attributes, skills, motivations and results. Sometimes scores drive a computer programme for pay purposes. Sometimes they are simply used to label people.

The numbers are arbitrary, often made worse by the practice of aggregating scores. On a ten-point scale, someone who scores 0 on one attribute and 10 on another averages 5. A score of five may qualify for an overall 'acceptable' label, yet the person really needs feedback to make a massive improvement in one domain, yet be seen as an exemplar to colleagues in the other.

One could be forgiven for feeling that management hasn't progressed far since the 1830s. At this time the followers of Jeremy Bentham, the philosopher and social reformer, measured the number of cesspits as an indicator of ill-health, the number of pubs as an indicator of immorality, and children's ability to recite hymns as an indicator of their religiousness!

THEME 7 QUESTIONNAIRE: ARE YOU MAKING YOUR NUMBERS COUNT?

ASSESSMENT

Write in empty boxes, complete statements, circle options, or tick where applicable. Numbers equate to points scored. In some of the questions the scores 0 – 3 are reversed.

7.1 How much importance does your organisation attach to numbers as the measure of success?

Don't know | 0. None | 1. Too little | 3. Right amount | 1. Too much

7.2 How much value does your organisation place in number crunchers at the top of the organisation?

Don't know | 0. None | 1. Too little | 3. Right amount | 1. Too much

7.3 How transparent a picture can be obtained from your company's accounts?

Don't know | 0. Not at all | 1. A little | 2. Fairly | 3. Very

7.4 How flexibly compiled are budgets?

Don't know | 0. Not at all | 1. A little | 2. Fairly | 3. Very

7.5 How honestly compiled are budgets?

Don't know | 0. Not at all | 1. A little | 2. Fairly | 3. Very

7.6 How flexibly applied are budgets?

Don't know | 0. Not at all | 1. A little | 2. Fairly | 3. Very

7.7 How inclined is your organisation to regard things as overly important because they are measurable?

Don't know | 3. Not at all | 2. A little | 1. Fairly | 0. Very

Give examples:

7.8 How inclined are you personally to regard things as overly important because they are measurable?

Don't know | 3. Not at all | 2. A little | 1. Fairly | 0. Very

Give examples:

7.9 How inclined is your organisation to disregard things because they are not measurable?

Don't know   3. Not at all   2. A little   1. Fairly   0. Very

Give examples:

7.10 How inclined are you personally to disregard things because they are not measurable?

Don't know   3. Not at all   2. A little   1. Fairly   0. Very

Give examples:

7.11 How often does your organisation use numbers pseudo-scientifically to lend spurious credibility to a policy, assessment, result, etc?

Don't know   3. Not at all   2. A little   1. Fairly   0. Very

Give examples:

7.12 How often do you personally use numbers pseudo-scientifically to lend spurious credibility to a policy, assessment, result, etc?

Don't know   3. Not at all   2. A little   1. Fairly   0. Very

Give examples:

7.13 How frequently are your department's numbers altered by others to present a more favourable picture?

Don't know   3. Not at all   2. A little   1. Fairly   0. Very

Give examples:

7.14 How frequently are your department's numbers altered by you to present a more favourable picture?

Don't know 3. Not at all 2. A little 1. Fairly 0. Very

Give examples:

7.15 How frequently are you on the receiving end of management numbers that stretch credulity?

Don't know 3. Not at all 2. A little 1. Fairly 0. Very

7.16 How significant are your organisation's intangible assets? *(No points)*

Don't know	Not at all	A little	Fairly	Very
☐	☐	☐	☐	☐

7.17 What important but intangible assets would benefit if ways could be found of measuring them?

7.18 Does your organisation use numbers to rank individuals' performance against colleagues?

Don't know 3. Not at all 2. A little 1. Fairly 0. Very

7.19 Does your organisation use numbers to summarise individuals' overall performance?

Don't know 3. Not at all 2. A little 1. Fairly 0. Very

SCORING

Total number of points scored ☐

Out of a possible maximum of 51

Percentage = ☐ %

Theme 7: Management by Numbers

REFLECTIONS

Capture your observations, thoughts and ideas here.

Good ideas that I have picked up:

Important things that my organisation should do:

Urgent things that my organisation should do:

Things that I can and should do myself:

Things that I need to investigate further:

Things that I need to discuss with other people (say whom):

THEME 8: CHANGE MANAGEMENT

Organisations have a tendency to try to force order out of chaos by focusing entirely on the legitimate system. The effect is to generate resistance. An enriched understanding of the shadow side enables managers to be more successful in managing change and bringing about improvement. It helps them to:

- become aware of how the shadow side can stop planned change in its tracks, obstructing managers from making rational change
- directly target dysfunctional features of the shadow side when making organisation change or improvement interventions
- recognise the interconnectedness of the legitimate system and the shadow system when intervening to make improvements

Different approaches

As we stated at the outset, some psychologists refer to the shadow side, while others speak of the shadow system. But differences are more than linguistic.

Egan portrays the organisation's two halves as rational and non-rational. He views personal features in the shadow side as likely either to constrain or to assist the organisation when attempting to bring about change. Furthermore, the organisation's culture (the over-riding shadow-side element) may be generally supportive or obstructive in facilitating change.

Bentley expresses it slightly differently. He takes an 'holistic' view – i.e. seeing the whole organisation. The legitimate and shadow systems are more than different and complementary: they are connected and overlap. In the context of managing change, the two systems need to be considered together so that a positive balance can exist between them.

The legitimate system

The legitimate system embodies the aims, purpose and values of the organisation as espoused and understood by its leaders or authority figures. In the legitimate system people operate in conformity with the established culture. They do things the 'way that things are done around here'.

This is the way the organisation claims to understand its culture and wishes to present it. It's how an induction programme might tell recruits 'this is how we do things round here' (with the implied 'and we expect you to comply'). This might be less than the full picture as seen by those not in authority. When recruits later join their department, they may be told that they can forget what's they've been told and 'this is what really happens'.

The shadow system

This system is more obscure. People participate in ways that serve their own needs rather than those of their organisation. This is the system that supports people in being who they are rather than how the organisation needs them to be.

In this view, the canteen is not just for eating. So-called 'canteen culture' gives life and energy to the shadow system. Among other things, it permits the exchange of gossip about the legitimate system and those in authority. Ironically, the legitimate system may be a few yards away, represented by the curtained-off senior managers' dining area!

A healthy organisation finds ways of legitimising discussion of things talked about in the canteen culture of the shadow system. In overly formal systems these issues remain undiscussed and undiscussible.

Overlapping systems

The two systems overlap. The nature and the amount of overlap can vary, as can whether the two systems are joined (a healthy condition) or one is eclipsing the other as in a solar eclipse (an unhealthy loss of light).

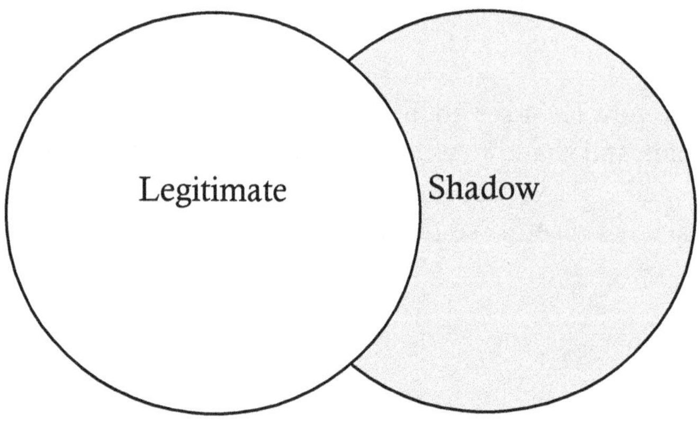

- If the shadow system is eclipsed by the legitimate system it might mean that people are constrained by an autocratic regime.

- If the shadow system dominates and eclipses the legitimate system, it is more likely that anarchy reigns.

- If the two systems are far apart, the organisation may disintegrate.
- If there is a lot of overlap, then the shadow system is supportive of the legitimate system.
- If there is a little overlap, the shadow system may be pressing for change.

WILDCAT STRIKE

In 2003, British Airways' check-in agents took sudden unofficial strike action when faced with a new electronic timekeeping system. Insufficient communication in the legitimate system had led to its breaking down and losing control to the shadow system, which took over communication. The shadow system also suffered a breakdown as the unions tried to regain control and make any strike action official. Attempts by the legitimate system to eclipse the shadow system failed. The shadow system gained visibility through media attention and eclipsed the legitimate system.

Change interventions

The majority of change initiatives in organisations are aimed at the legitimate system. But without the support of the shadow system, it is unlikely that the changes will be successful.

The shadow system provides people with a safe place to develop their resistance to the demands of the legitimate system. Because of this, systemic interventions need to be directed at both the legitimate system and the shadow system, claims Bentley:

> *'If the needs of the shadow system are ignored, it is likely that the interventions will push the shadow system much closer to anarchy than it currently might be.'*

The case study below describes a retailer's change process. The company, Halfords, was undergoing a revamp and was experiencing staff unrest. With the advice and assistance of Ashridge Consulting Ltd it successfully used unorthodox techniques with employees at all levels.

HALFORDS

In 2000, Halfords was embarking on a period of change. The UK's largest retailer of car parts, cycles and associated leisure products, was revamping its 400-plus outlets and introducing new approaches in head office, but staff felt disenfranchised. In the warehouse industrial action had only been narrowly avoided, and the atmosphere was one of control and conformity.

... Instead of getting stuck in the traditional mindset which says that organisations are like machines – so that all that is needed are the right 'levers', a plan and a timetable of implementation – Ashridge Consulting prefers an ongoing dialogue.

... The technique [known as 'appreciative enquiry'] demands that managers abandon the illusion of executive omnipotence. Traditionally, managers like to give the impression that they are able to control, or steer the cultures of their businesses. But with appreciative enquiry everyone gets involved in the process, and both staff and managers must admit that there is no set goal before setting out on their journey.

... In one workshop event the warehouse team acted on a long-standing issue. They got together over tea and called for the removal of the warehouse's most disliked feature – a buzzer that controlled their breaks. One of the guys stood up and said, 'We are gong in tomorrow and we are going to rip out the buzzer', [adding a pledge] 'we will always be where we need to be when we need to be there'.

... the 'pull' approach ... of working with conversation, storytelling and relationship has enabled a new culture to start to develop. It is based on the idea of lighting a few small fires (rather than the usual 'big bang' type change initiative). Some of them will go out and you assume that they were not supposed to catch in the first place, but the ones that catch alight will spread faster and soon everything is ablaze.

Abridged from 'A little more conversation', Management Consultancies Association Awards 2003, *The Guardian,* 06 February 2003

Ossification versus disintegration

Everything is constantly changing, a point often not understood, according to Bentley. Order is inevitably followed by disturbance and a period of chaos, which in turn is followed by the creation of a new order. Any attempt to resist this 'dance of life' leads to ossification and/or disintegration.

Ossification occurs when the old order is rigidly maintained using an increasingly doctrinaire legitimate system. The inflexible demand for conformity causes people to contract; creativity dies, and the organisation withers away.

Disintegration occurs when the shadow system is so far removed from the legitimate system that the two cannot be reunited. People become so expanded and diverse in the shadow system that the legitimate system no longer holds any value or purpose for them and so it and the organisation die.

The twin dangers of ossification and disintegration can be avoided by judicious interventions in both the legitimate and shadow systems.

THEME 8 QUESTIONNAIRE: ARE YOU CHANGING THE SHADOW OR CHANGING WITH THE SHADOW?

ASSESSMENT

Write in empty boxes, complete statements, circle options, or tick where applicable. Numbers equate to points scored. In some of the questions the scores 0 – 3 are reversed.

In your organisation

8.1 How much awareness is there of the shadow system's ability to influence change?

Don't know	0. None	1. A little	2. Some	3. Considerable

8.2 How much respect is there for the shadow system's ability to influence change?

Don't know	0. None	1. A little	2. Some	3. Considerable

8.3 How much respect is there for the shadow system's unofficial 'legitimacy'?

Don't know	0. None	1. A little	2. Some	3. Considerable

8.4 How strong is the propensity to attempt change entirely through the rational/legitimate system?

Don't know	3. Not at all	2. A little	1. Fairly	0. Very

8.5 How strong is the propensity to overlook the shadow system when attempting change?

Don't know	3. Not at all	2. A little	1. Fairly	0. Very

8.6 How strong is the propensity to ride roughshod over the shadow system when attempting change?

Don't know	3. Not at all	2. A little	1. Fairly	0. Very

8.7 How much practical account is taken of the shadow system when attempting change?

Don't know	0. None	1. A little	2. Some	3. Considerable

8.8 How much harmony is there currently between the legitimate and shadow system?

Don't know	0. None	1. A little	2. Some	3. Considerable

8.9 How well suited is the dominant management style to working with the shadow system in facilitating change?

Don't know	0. Not at all	1. A little	2. Fairly	3. Very

You personally

8.10 How aware are you personally of the shadow system's ability to influence change?

Don't know	0. Not at all	1. A little	2. Fairly	3. Considerably

8.11 How much respect have you for the shadow system's ability to influence change?

Don't know	0. None	1. A little	2. Some	3. Considerable

8.12 How much respect have you for the shadow system's unofficial 'legitimacy'?

Don't know	0. None	1. A little	2. Some	3. Considerable

8.13 How strong is your propensity to attempt change entirely through the rational/legitimate system?

Don't know	3. Not at all	2. A little	1. Fairly	0. Very

8.14 How strong is your propensity to forget the shadow system when attempting change?

Don't know	3. Not at all	2. A little	1. Fairly	0. Very

8.15 How strong is your propensity to ride roughshod over the shadow system when attempting change?

Don't know	3. Not at all	2. A little	1. Fairly	0. Very

8.16 How much do you take practical account of the shadow system when attempting change?

Don't know	0. None	1. A little	2. Some	3. Considerable

8.17 How well suited is your own management style to working with the shadow system in facilitating change?

Don't know	0. Not at all	1. A little	2. Fairly	3. Very

8.18 How well do you understand the organisation's true culture?

Don't know	0. Not at all	1. A little	2. Fairly	3. Very

8.19 How close to your own perception is the official portrayal of the organisation's culture?

Don't know	0. Not at all	1. A little	2. Fairly	3. Very

8.20 How strong is your own demand for people to conform to the legitimate system?

Don't know	3. Not at all	2. A little	1. Fairly	0. Very

8.21 How aware are you of the natural cycle between disturbance and the creation of a new order?

Don't know	0. Not at all	1. A little	2. Fairly	3. Very

SCORING

Your organisation

Total number of points scored ☐
Out of a possible maximum of 27
Percentage = ☐ %

Yourself

Total number of points scored ☐
Out of a possible maximum of 36
Percentage = ☐ %

Total number of points scored ☐
Out of a possible maximum of 63
Percentage = ☐ %

Where the same question is repeated, first for your organisation and then for yourself, you may wish to check whether you personally are ahead of or behind the organisation generally.

THEME 8: CHANGE MANAGEMENT

REFLECTIONS

Capture your observations, thoughts and ideas here.

Good ideas that I have picked up:

Important things that my organisation should do:

Urgent things that my organisation should do:

Things that I can and should do myself:

Things that I need to investigate further:

Things that I need to discuss with other people (say whom):

Theme 9: Organisation Culture

Culture is the most powerful and controlling of all the shadow-side factors. Culture affects not only overt organisational behaviour, but also shadow-side behaviour, such as how crazy or idiosyncratic people can be. Despite its importance, culture cannot be determined by examining company documents and policy statements; hence its location in the shadow side of the organisational equation.

Culture lays down shadow-side norms, such as:

- whether you have to be an accountant to get the top job
- what kind of clothes are deemed appropriate to wear
- how much bullying by bosses is OK to get things done
- whether power is blatant or subtle
- how much individuality is tolerated
- whether or not the same conventions and injunctions as for everyone else apply at the top
- whether email dominates communication, even between adjacent desks
- the degree of competitiveness – internally and externally

Competition and collaboration

Competition and collaboration are a basic and essential characteristic of people (individuals and natural groups and tribes) and business organisations. They are essential features of all organisations. They are manifested in both external and internal relationships. But rarely are they in harmony.

The shadow-side comes to the fore when there is an excess and dysfunctional level – more often of competition than collaboration, and more often channelled internally towards (or against) colleagues rather than business competitors. A wide range of shadow-side behaviour (e.g. greed, ambition, envy) is revealed when there is a strong desire to dominate and win – often at someone else's expense.

External competition is less likely to be viewed as excessive and qualify for the shadow-side label; though such instances abound; e.g. negative advertising, industrial espionage, stealing a competitor's customers, and engaging in price wars.

Internal competition is often manifested in inter-departmental rivalry. A good example comes from BBC Radio.

THE ENEMY WITHIN

David Liddament, the outgoing ITV boss at the time (August 2002), questioned what the BBC was for. Eddie Mair, a BBC broadcaster, replied as follows:-

"The BBC is there to do what it has always done. Take on the common enemy. Each other. You may hear Today, and The World at One and PM all coming out of the radio on the same channel, Radio 4. But make no mistake. Although we all work for the same network, we are in different departments within BBC News – quite deliberately so – to ensure that we have to compete, and to keep our journalism sharp.

Because our rivals on Today and The World Tonight can read PM's running order on the communal computer system, we go out of our way to make the stories look as incomprehensible as possible. Editors often give stories joke names. A brutal assault on a pensioner might become 'Bashed Up Granny' in the running order. A particularly inept policy initiative might become 'Hopeless'. It could be argued that this is merely part of the dark humour that lurks in all newsrooms. It could also be the product of very sick minds. I really don't care.

We don't even put names of guests in the running order any more. If we've secured a Peter Mandelson interview, he simply appears as 'P'. Similarly, Theresa May is 'T', and Dame Judi Dench is 'M'.

When new producers arrive with us from Today or The World Tonight, they are asked, informally, if they still have computer access to their old contact lists. If they say yes, they are taken to a windowless eight-foot-square room with a table, two chairs and a light bulb and debriefed until they're whimpering. And that's just the job interview.

The point is, though, that rivalry between different departments within the BBC is far greater than that directed towards different broadcasters. We at World at One and PM are far more interested in what the Today programme is doing than what commercial radio is up to."

Extract from Eddie Mair: 'The enemy within', *The Guardian,* 21 August 2002

The BBC example shows how powerful is the human need to compete in what may seem to be bizarre ways and in a context that appears to be counter-productive to the interests of the institution as a whole. Internal competition becomes more than interpersonal rivalry: it becomes one of the work unit's norms, part of its own microculture. New arrivals are inducted into these departmental values and habits.

At first glance this seems crazy. Wouldn't the BBC be better off if such intense and localised competition was focused on the outside enemy (commercial radio and television) and replaced with internal collaboration?

While the BBC case may seem amusing, some companies practise a much darker form of internal competition. Enron, the disgraced US energy trading company famously employed a policy called 'rank and yank'.

RANK AND YANK

Senior Enron managers were required annually to rank all their staff . The lowest 10% automatically lost their jobs. This was despite the fact that the company recruited the best talent from the country's top universities. The motive behind the cruel approach was to use fear and insecurity to drive the employees to perform highly and compete vigorously. The dysfunctional policy did not help Enron avoid bankruptcy.

Upsides and downsides of competition

John Varney, Director of the Centre for Management Creativity, bemoans the fact that the word 'competition' fails to distinguish between what he describes as the "aspiration to learn from others in order to excel" and "the desire to do others down for material gain".

GOING TO THE WALL

An airline's reorganisation deliberately left fuzzy departmental boundaries and presented opportunities for pairs of departments to believe that they had duplicated responsibilities. The idea was that they would try to excel, and the better one would survive.

This internal competition idea can be taken further: it may be believed that an organisation needs to progress through this phase of internal competition before it can have the right spirit to take on the external enemy.

NATIONAL FREIGHT CORPORATION

The National Freight Corporation were concerned that their staff lacked sufficient competitive instinct to do battle with their external competitors. They believed that their staff could not distinguish between different targets to which to apply their competitive instincts. The company controversially decided that the route to competing externally was via first competing internally. They would not be able to get one without the other, and would therefore need to artificially stimulate internal competition.

The above company's conclusion may have sprung from evidence that some of us appear to be naturally competitive whatever the context, while others are far less so. However:

- While it is true that some people are much more competitive than others and appear to need to win at everything they do, people do generally appear able to behave collaboratively within what they see as their own family group, and to reserve competition for those outside the group.
- You can provoke internal conflict more easily than you can turn it off.
- Internal competition can be directed in a number of directions: over 'turf' (unhealthy); over resources and jobs (natural); over ideas (an asset).

Professionals' fees

Building upon what we said earlier under 'Target Setting', an area in which the use of targets is common is that of setting highly demanding levels of billable hours in the legal and accountancy professions. The practice is deeply embedded in most firms' culture. Yet such practice risks distorting people's working practices, compromising customer service, as well as putting personal values under strain.

A survey conducted in November 2002 by *Accountancy Age* magazine revealed that 80% of UK financial directors believed that bills from accountants and auditors had been padded.

TARGETS FOR BILLABLE HOURS

"The firm's requirement that its associates bill 2,420 hours per year – about 48 hours per week – was 'profoundly unrealistic", lawyers wrote in a memo to the firm's partnership. ... The requirement "angers, worries and harries virtually every associate in the firm," the memo said. An associate said the target was "totally ludicrous, offensive and generally makes me crazy". ('Lawyers say Clifford Chance works them too hard', ***Forbes*** **magazine, 28 October 2002)**

'... the country's biggest accountancy firm [UK's Pricewaterhouse Coopers] admitted that it set tough 'utilisation targets' for client-facing staff. The news comes after firms were warned to be wary of bill padding following the publication of a memo from lawyers at City law firm Clifford Chance complaining of "dehumanising conditions" that "promote padding of hours" by staff. ... Utilisation targets for client-facing staff ranged from 70% of time spent working on client affairs for a junior executive to 55% for a senior manager. ... Some staff inside the firm are concerned about the pressures created by dealing with the targets – understood to be analysed on a fortnightly basis and a contributory factor in the calculation of bonuses.' ('Bill padding row reaches accountants', ***Accountancy Age,*** **21 November 2002)**

'A former KPMG employee, who asked not to be named, said: "Chargeable hour targets were the be-all and end-all of the job, and were analysed monthly. The pressures to meet these targets led to huge temptations to pad bills. Two-minute phone calls would be put down for quarter of an hour. In meetings with clients you would charge for any chit-chat at the beginning and end." ' ('KPMG does utilisation target u-turn', ***Accountancy Age,*** **12 December 2002)**

Management consulting

Jokes abound about the culture of management consultancies. The values of some are decidedly dark.

FROM BAD TO WORSE

A productivity consultancy's business model was based on conducting a short initial datagathering and analysis of a client's business for a nominal fee. At the end of this the senior partner would make a presentation to the client's board of management. At the presentation, regardless of the evidence of the data, he would claim that the business was in a far more parlous state than had been imagined. In fact, it probably could not be saved from collapse. But he would claim that just occasionally the consultants had seen chinks of light that gave him the merest hope, and it was probably worth trying to save the company before it was too late. Their fee for saving the company would be £xm ...

Social norms

Most companies have social norms, tightly prescribed or loosely understood, but rarely enunciated. Michael Maxtone-Graham ('Put a mentor in your manual', *Training*, 1991) published the following list [here abbreviated] as an indicative guide:-

TABLE 5 SOME SOCIAL NORMS
• When you succeed, share the credit with others. • If you must drink at lunch, have only one. • If you don't know the answer to a question, say so. • If you make a mistake, admit it. • If you offend someone, apologise. • Stay well groomed. • Remember people's names. • Don't discuss salary with your peers. • Be nice to people you don't like. • Try very hard not to say, "I told you so".

The consultancy division of a large accountancy firm had a "culture of civility, but it was a veneer" (Gerard Egan, *Working the Shadow Side,* 1994). Although it seemed like a nice place to work, behind the façade was another set of less appetising norms. A selection appears in Table 6:

TABLE 6 COVERT NORMS
• Share dirt on just about anyone, but not the CEO. He has a way of finding out who said what about him, and he will get you. • Take as much credit as you can when things go well, but do it subtly. • Get to know someone in the boss's office. You'll find out early which way the wind is blowing, and this will help you make a good appearance. • Don't let people get away with things. Send signals early on that you know how to retaliate. "Don't tread on me" is not a bad motto around here. • On the other hand don't make enemies unless you have to. Enemies around here are a big burden.

The consequence of these norms was that everyone was always on their guard. People couldn't relax. It was a tough culture for a tough culture, but it didn't serve the business well.

Culture of perfectionism

Some organisations embody a culture of perfectionism. Everything needs to be done to a high standard even if it no longer adds value to the business. The explanation underlying the practice might itself lie in the culture, where people are fearful, insecure and risk averse.

> A group had done eight dry runs for one presentation and more were scheduled. They had developed 45 slides for the presentation, but had over 200 in reserve so that every possible question could be answered.
>
> (Gerard Egan: 'The shadow side', *Management Today*, September 1993)

The norms which drive this behaviour included 'Beware of committing career-interrupting mistakes' and 'Find out what's in your boss's mind in order to tailor your choice of projects and their presentation'.

Ploys

Business strategies take many forms. According to the strategy guru Henry Mintzberg, strategies may be policies, plans, perspectives, patterns and ploys. The first four items sit comfortably within our expectations of rationality. But ploy is pure shadow side. Some organisations are renowned for them.

FORKED TONGUES

A corporation that proclaims support for the environment and works with pressure groups may be engaging in a ploy. The aim may be to divert attention and deflect criticism. Directors of the disgraced US energy trading company Enron were assiduous as philanthropists and at building the company's image as a good employer and corporate citizen, while engaging in accountancy tricks which left the company bankrupt and employees without pensions.

Email culture

Once expected to be a minority interest for technocrats, email is having a pervasive effect on office workers' lives. The ease with which people can be include in emails means that some people may have hundreds of emails to deal with when they turn up for work, especially after a weekend. Email so dominates people's working lives that the subject is spawning an email culture.

The ease and practicality of email comes with an easy attitude that affects the language. Some companies feel a need to monitor (i.e. censor) employees' emails for foul language and prejudicial remarks that they believe could lead to a company being sued by an aggrieved employee slighted or offended. Some companies put in place screening software on incoming emails to protect their employees' sensibilities from swear words. Such action may say more about the managers' own attitudes towards swear words and view of their role as censors than about the staff and their need to be protected.

The advent of email is undermining hierarchies and fostering networks that are independent of physical office proximity. The youthful and apparently democratic nature of emails leads some chief executives to make public their email address to all their employees (the standard format for a given organisation may make this obvious anyway). They may then invite anyone in the organisation to email them about any concerns (notwithstanding that they may employ someone to filter or deal with their emails for them).

CAREER-LIMITING EMAILS

A newly appointed chief executive to a Swiss engineering conglomerate announced his email address and said he would be happy to receive emails from anyone in the company. A consultant working with the company cited this as a welcome development and indication of a new style of management. A manager responded that he would not dare: if his immediate superior found out that he had bypassed the chain of command to communicate directly with the chief executive, that would be a career-limiting move. The chief executive remained unaware of why he received few emails.

While email may have a dramatic effect on 'the way things are done around here' (organisation culture), some aspects of the culture will remain deeply entrenched and take much longer to change, as this example shows.

THEME 9 QUESTIONNAIRE: IS YOUR CULTURE SERVING YOUR BUSINESS WELL?

ASSESSMENT

Write in empty boxes, complete statements, circle options, or tick where applicable. Numbers equate to points scored. In some of the questions the scores 0 – 3 are reversed.

How rational is your organisation's culture in respect of the following:-

9.1 The ease with which talent from diverse backgrounds can rise to the most senior levels?

Don't know | 0. Not at all | 1. A little | 2. Fairly | 3. Very

9.2 The amount of tolerance shown to eccentrics?

Don't know | 0. Not at all | 1. A little | 2. Fairly | 3. Very

9.3 The freedom with which people can wear what they choose?

Don't know | 0. Not at all | 1. A little | 2. Fairly | 3. Very

9.4 The quality of decisions taken on logical grounds?

Don't know | 0. Not at all | 1. A little | 2. Fairly | 3. Very

9.5 The invoking of power explicitly on the basis of rank?

Don't know | 3. Not at all | 2. A little | 1. Fairly | 0. Very

9.6 The need to put everything in writing to 'cover your back'?

Don't know | 3. Not at all | 2. A little | 1. Fairly | 0. Very

9.7 The high number of issues that are undiscussible?

Don't know | 3. Not at all | 2. A little | 1. Fairly | 0. Very

9.8 The hiring of consultants as 'temporary employees' to get round a ban on consultants?

Don't know | 3. Not at all | 2. A little | 1. Fairly | 0. Very

9.9 The need to belong to a privileged clique or in-group?

Don't know | 3. Not at all | 2. A little | 1. Fairly | 0. Very

9.10 The value managers place on people's expressed opinions according to their grade?

Don't know | 3. Not at all | 2. A little | 1. Fairly | 0. Very

9.11 The striving to over-engineer everything to perfection beyond the point where it adds value?

Don't know | 3. Not at all | 2. A little | 1. Fairly | 0. Very

9.12 The punishing of failure by those who took a risk when encouraged and told safe to do so?

Don't know | 3. Not at all | 2. A little | 1. Fairly | 0. Very

9.13	The degree to which those at the top of the organisation don't consider that the rules apply to them too? Don't know 3. Not at all 2. A little 1. Fairly 0. Very
9.14	The high frequency with which people speak of there being a hidden agenda? Don't know 3. Not at all 2. A little 1. Fairly 0. Very
9.15	The extent of criticism of decisions on the grounds of their being unethical? Don't know 3. Not at all 2. A little 1. Fairly 0. Very
9.16	The amount of secrecy, especially over bosses' pay? Don't know 3. Not at all 2. A little 1. Fairly 0. Very
9.17	The level of stress and burnout? Don't know 3. Not at all 2. A little 1. Fairly 0. Very
9.18	The use of euphemisms (e.g. 'challenge' for 'difficulty', 'partners' for 'employees')? Don't know 3. Not at all 2. A little 1. Fairly 0. Very

Competition and collaboration: your organisation

9.19	How healthy is the internal competition? Don't know 0. Not at all 1. A little 2. Fairly 3. Very How does unhealthy internal competition manifest itself?
9.20	How healthy is the internal collaboration? Don't know 0. Not at all 1. A little 2. Fairly 3. Very How does unhealthy internal collaboration manifest itself?
9.21	How healthy is the external competition? Don't know 0. Not at all 1. A little 2. Fairly 3. Very How does unhealthy external competition manifest itself?
9.22	How healthy is the external collaboration? Don't know 0. Not at all 1. A little 2. Fairly 3. Very How does unhealthy external collaboration manifest itself?

Competition and collaboration: you personally

9.23

How inclined are you personally towards an excess of internal competitive spirit?				
Don't know	3. Not at all	2. A little	1. Fairly	0. Very

9.24

How inclined are you towards an excess of external competitive spirit?				
Don't know	3. Not at all	2. A little	1. Fairly	0. Very

9.25

How inclined are you towards too little internal collaborative spirit?				
Don't know	3. Not at all	2. A little	1. Fairly	0. Very

9.26

How inclined are you towards too little external collaborative spirit?				
Don't know	3. Not at all	2. A little	1. Fairly	0. Very

Email culture

9.27

How much is dealing with 'floods of emails' excessively dominating people's working time?				
Don't know	3. None	2. A little	1. Some	0. Considerably

9.28

How much is an email culture replacing face-to-face discourse?				
Don't know	3. None	2. A little	1. Some	0. Considerably

9.29

How much awareness is there that there is a shadow side to the use of emails?				
Don't know	0. None	1. A little	2. Some	3. Considerable

9.30

How much concern is there over potential misuse of emails?				
Don't know	0. None	1. A little	2. Some	3. Considerable

9.31

How much concern is there over possible bad language or offensive remarks in emails?				
Don't know	0. None	1. A little	2. Some	3. Considerable

9.32

How much effort is going into setting standards, policies, norms for sound email usage?				
Don't know	0. None	1. A little	2. Some	3. Considerable

9.33

How much anxiety exists over management's censoring and disciplining staff for email 'offences'?				
Don't know	3. None	2. A little	1. Some	0. Considerable

SCORING

Total number of points scored	☐
Out of a possible maximum of	99
Percentage =	☐ %

THEME 9: ORGANISATION CULTURE

REFLECTIONS

Capture your observations, thoughts and ideas here.

Good ideas that I have picked up:

Important things that my organisation should do:

Urgent things that my organisation should do:

Things that I can and should do myself:

Things that I need to investigate further:

Things that I need to discuss with other people (say whom):

CASE STUDY
WHITEMOOR PRISON

To learn more about managing the shadow side we shall dissect a major organisational failure, a high-profile prison breakout. Prisons, and the UK Government's Prison Service, provide some of the most vivid illustrations of the shadow side, as well as failure by politicians and officials to observe it, understand it and manage it. One particular example of a breakout is well documented: the escape by five high-risk Category A prisoners (IRA and Mafia) in 1994 from Whitemoor in Cambridgeshire.

The shadow side was prevalent at three levels:

1. day-to-day management in the prisons before the breakouts happened
2. the response by the Prison Service to try to prevent future breakouts
3. the interplay between officials and Government ministers as those with responsibility sought to avoid being blamed.

THE STORY OF THE WHITEMOOR PRISON BREAKOUT

The prison already had sophisticated cameras which could cover the whole perimeter. It had arrangements for visitors to pass through metal detector portals. It scanned their belongings so they could be viewed on a monitor. It tape-recorded prisoners' phone calls. It trained officers to conduct thorough 'rub-down' body searches. It had a Board of Visitors to regularly inspect and report their findings to the governor and prison service management.

In the light of an enquiry after the escape, the Home Secretary announced the following additional action:-

1. **Introduce a more systematic method of recording intelligence and security information on staff.**
2. **Issue high-security unit staff with personal alarms**
3. **Reinforce the walls and fences.**

Along with the inevitable calls for more training came the equally predictable memos to officers reminding them of their duties and responsibilities. The memo from the Director-General called for the following action:-

1. **Ensure that all ladders are stored securely.**
2. **Ensure that all tools are accounted for daily.**
3. **Ensure that loose items that could be stacked against the perimeter fence to aid climbing are either fixed or located in an area where they cannot be effectively used.**
4. **Use ground and fence patrols to prevent escapes as frequently as resources allow.**
5. **Search effectively cells, prisoners, visitors and items entering the establishment.**

This is all highly rational and good common sense. But does it reach the heart of the problem? The answer is No. We learn that:

- **One or more cameras were left static as a matter of conscious practice (if not explicit policy), leaving a blind spot by the perimeter fence. Why? Because some of the betterconnected prisoners complained that it was an invasion of privacy!**
- **The cassette tapes were turned over to erase and re-record over the previous conversation and were not played back.**
- **The principal Mafia convict was allowed to talk in Italian, and none of the officers could understand what he was saying.**
- **The metal detector had been installed near pipes and had to have its sensitivity reduced to avoid false alarms, so it no longer detected visitors' metal objects.**
- **The officer who should have been watching the X-ray monitor had to stand at the end of the conveyor belt to take the items off because there was no one else to do it.**
- **The inmates made curtains to put over the hobbies room windows so that the officers couldn't see them making escape ladders.**
- **Body searches were not carried out because it upset the high-security prisoners.**
- **These prisoners' possessions were so numerous that they could not practicably be searched; some of their adjacent cells were requisitioned as extra 'wardrobes'.**
- **Prisoners pushed the visiting room's doors shut when friends called, and the officers felt reluctant to open them.**
- **Written edicts were ignored, as were the concerned reports submitted by the Board of Visitors. Officers who could have been watching prisoners were out getting their shopping, buying the wealthier inmates Cromer crabs, fresh salmon and rare spices.**

The analysis and response was as predictable as it was misguided. There is nothing revelatory from the Director-General in his memo. It's already understood; it's simply not happening. The Home Secretary wanted to be seen to be taking action (spending money) in terms his public constituency (the electorate) could understand. But it missed the target. The Home Secretary and his management team were looking for rational answers to poorly understood irrational problems. But what happens in most organisations most of the time is not at all rational. To get to the truth you need to turn a few stones over and examine the organisation's darker, shadow side.

Extract from William Tate: *Developing Corporate Competence – A High-Performance Agenda for Managing Organizations,* Gower, 1995

The shadow-side elements included:

- Power struggles
- Trading of favour between officers and inmates
- Manipulating and conditioning officers to put them off their guard
- Corruption
- Management insecurity
- Fear of responsibility under the spotlight, especially at the top of the political ladder
- Prison officers' decisions countermanded when powerful prisoners appealed over
- their heads
- Party politicking to appeal to the electorate

- A bureaucracy replete with buck-passing and pulling the rug from under managers in the complex management chain between officers, governors, regional directors, the Director-General heading up the government agency, and numerous ministers and Home Office civil servants

Fingers were pointed at individuals, especially the prison governor, but he was the wrong target. It is a natural response to blame individuals when there are performance problems. But very often it is the gap between individuals, and between functional groups, that is the problem.

Managing the shadow side requires an honest and enlightened analysis to find out what is going on. Listing the rational and the non-rational factors in the system helps explain and understand what is happening. One can then see more clearly where to put energy and resources in attempting to come up with wise and enduring solutions.

An analysis of rational and non-rational factors operating at Whitemoor prison appears overleaf.

TABLE 7
ANALYSIS OF RATIONAL AND SHADOW FACTORS AT WHITEMOOR PRISON

Rational Factors	Shadow Factors
Governor announces new vision, including public statement that Special Security Unit is 100 per cent escape proof.	The Board of Visitors' reports are ignored.
	Instructions ignored in practice.
A Board of Visitors monitors and reports.	Cameras sometimes turned off. Cameras left static, creating a blindspot, because of 'invasion of privacy'.
Written edicts and exhortations by Governor.	Volume of possessions out of control (extra cellsused as wardrobes, and huge containers in yard).
Heavy expenditure on equipment. Cameras installed which can swivel 360 degrees.	Tapes not played back. Mafia man allowed to speak in Italian; no one can understand him. World-wide phone calls (at public expense).
Policy of regular searches.	One officer at end of conveyor belt taking things off; no one to watch the monitor.
Phone calls are tape recorded.	Turned down sensitivity of metal detector portal, because underground pipes close by.
Incoming deliveries to prisoners by visitors monitored by security screen on conveyor belt.	Visitors not body-searched, because inmates threaten violence.
Visitors pass through metal detector portal.	Prisoners push the door closed and officers dare not reopen it.
Officers trained in rub downs (body searches).	Naive and inexperienced young officers put in charge of high-risk category prisoners. Officers remain in contact with same prisoners for long periods of service.
Visitors meet prisoners in special room with officer to observe through open door.	Applied practice of appeasement and concessions. Widespread intimidation. Conditioning of officers. Psychological textbooks in cells. Wreaths sent to officers' homes. Bribery and corruption rife.
Policy of providing local employment for young unemployed persons.	
Claimed official policy of tough regime.	Prisoners issued with hacksaw blades to use in the hobbies room. Curtains drawn over window of hobbies room where escape equipment made.
	Staff act as lackeys for inmates, doing shopping.
	Officers overruled by governor. Governor overruled by Home Office. Regional directors blame all problems on the governors. Director General speaks of good 'industrial relations' with governors.

PLANNING IMPROVEMENT ACTION

Gap analysis

This self-assessment audit process has, in a sense, been a series of gap analyses. It has been helping you to search for, and identify, gaps between:

- the way senior management *think* the organisation works, and the way it works in practice
- what senior managers say and what they actually do
- your own approach and that of the organisation as a whole

It will have helped you focus on specific problems and gaps in the subjects covered by each of the nine themes.

Identifying and closing these gaps are crucially important activities – underpinning your organisation's culture, performance and (for most businesses) profitability.

We now look at gap analysis in a slightly different way, as a prelude to planning improvements and what may be change-management interventions. These are higher-order gaps that can get in the way of making changes. Understanding these gaps is crucial to being able to make changes stick.

This calls for openness, accuracy, honesty, imagination, political skill and leadership. Another audit, *The Organisational Leadership Audit,* may be helpful here.

Types of gap

When considering the process of change, relevant gaps to take into account include those between:

1. management's rhetoric and current organisation reality (*out of touch*)
2. management's rhetoric and privately held values and beliefs (*cynical*)
3. management's aspirations and present organisational state (*stretched*)
4. management's aspirations and current organisational reality (*unrealistic*)
5. management's aspirations and current organisational capacity to respond (*incapable*)

6. the organisational skills/resources needed and those available (*under-resourced*)

7. official targets and current performance (*wide*)

8. what the organisation needs to know and what it does know (*learning need*)

9. what the organisation doesn't know it needs to know (*blind spot*)

10. the organisation's legitimate system and shadow system (*politics*)

We suggest that you keep these types of gap in mind when understanding what lies behind the need to make changes, as well as when making plans, and when communicating with others about those plans.

Who owns the gap?

There is also the question of who 'owns' the gap and is therefore willing to take responsibility for doing something about it. If someone perceives there is a gap, but then expects someone else to close it, there is a risk of breaking the cycle through which people accept responsibility for taking remedial action and sense that they have personal control. (See diagram below.)

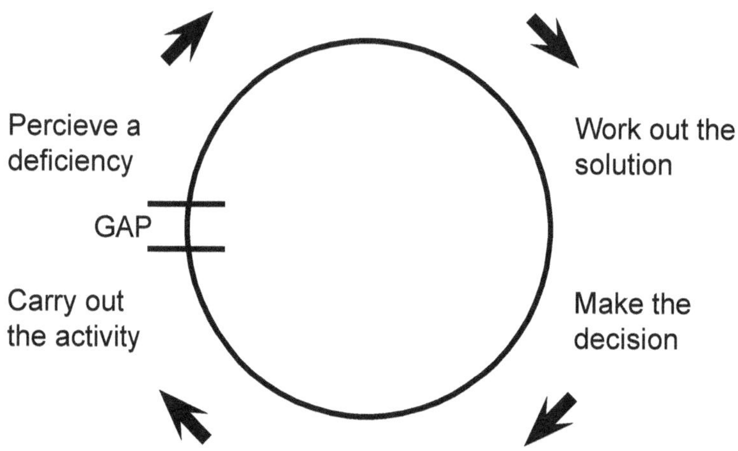

An analogy to the improvement cycle is found in the example of a thermostat. The mechanism that detects the temperature deficiency is directly connected with the booster pump or air conditioning fan. Contrast that with full-time quality inspectors in manufacturing whose job it is to inspect and reject *other people's work.*

Action planning

The following pages contain forms that are designed to help you develop practical plans. Once complete, you may want to copy them and put them in a prominent position as a ready reminder.

What and where is the problem?

As a result of conducting this audit:

How in touch is your organisation with its shadow side?

How powerful a feature is the shadow side in your organisation's life? In what way? Overall, is its impact generally positive or negative?

In what ways is the shadow side most negatively affecting your organisation's performance?

In what ways is the shadow side most positively affecting your organisation's performance?

Where in your organisation is successful management of the shadow side most vital?

Where is the shadow side currently not well managed but important, and therefore most in need of improvement?

How vulnerable is your organisation as a result of a failure to manage the shadow side?

What is making it difficult for your organisation to improve its management of the shadow side?

Addressing the need

Which of the audit's nine themes offer substantial scope for tackling current negative shadow-side issues in your organisation? You may wish to indicate which have the highest priority.

Themes		
Aware and concerned about:	Can help	Priority
1. Office politics	☐	☐
2. Trust and relationships	☐	☐
3. Training and development	☐	☐
4. Creativity and innovation	☐	☐
5. Reward and punishment	☐	☐
6. Target setting	☐	☐
7. Management by numbers	☐	☐
8. Change management	☐	☐
9. Organisation culture	☐	☐

What are the various actions that you think the organisation should take?

Important action:

Urgent action:

What are the various actions that you personally should take?

Important action:

Urgent action:

Which action points are 'quick hits' where improvement can be achieved most easily?

What can you do on your own authority, and what must you seek consent for?

Who needs to be involved in sharing your conclusions?

Who are the main stakeholders affected by improvement plans?

Who most needs to be involved in planning improvement action?

What obstacles lie in the path of making changes?

What further expertise or resources would be helpful?

Be clear who are your friends and enemies

You are likely to need to marshal support for your plans, as well as counter any opposition. When you want to get something important agreed to, recognise that the pure merit of your case may well be insufficient to persuade some of your colleagues. Some of them may oppose your arguments because they don't like you. Or they may support your argument because they support you, even though they do not like your idea. So conduct a private analysis beforehand of where people stand with respect to you and to your idea. This will help you sort out who to lobby – either to support you, or to support your idea, according to where their sympathies lie.

Write the names of the key players in the appropriate boxes.

1. For you personally / For your ideas	2. Against you personally / For your ideas
3. For you personally / Against your ideas	4. Against you personally / Against your ideas

Definitions and strategies:

1. Who can be relied upon to back you personally and to agree with your proposals?
   (Don't spend a lot of time explaining your proposals to these people.)

2. Who will oppose you personally, but will agree with your proposals?
   (Spend time trying to improve your relationship with these people.)

3. Who will back you personally, but may not agree with your proposals?
   (Spend time trying to convince them of the merits of the planned change.)

4. Who will oppose your proposals, and cannot be relied upon to support you personally either?
   (Don't waste time trying to persuade these people.)

REFERENCES

1. Trevor Bentley: 'The emerging system: A gestalt approach to organisational interventions', *British Gestalt Journal,* Vol 10, No.1, pp 13-19

2. David Boyle: *The Tyranny of Numbers – Why Counting Can't Make Us Happy,* HarperCollins, 2001

3. Simon Caulkin: 'An end to the numbers game', *The Observer,* 13 April 2003

4. Gerard Egan: *Working the Shadow Side,* San Francisco: Jossey-Bass, 1994

5. Gerard Egan: 'Managing the shadow side in an organisation' (ch.) in *Adding Value: A Systematic Guide to Business-Driven Management and Leadership,* San Francisco: Jossey Bass, 1993

6. Gerard Egan: 'The Shadow Side', *Management Today,* September 1993

7. Alfie Kohn: *Punished by Rewards,* New York: Houghton Mifflin, 1993

8. Ralph D. Stacey: *Complexity and Creativity in Organizations,* San Francisco: Berrett-Koehler, 1996

9. William Tate: *Demerging Organisations,* London: Financial Times Management, Pearson Education, 1999

10. William Tate: *Developing Corporate Competence – A High-Performance Agenda for Managing Organizations,* Aldershot: Gower 1995

11. John Varney: 'Competing for the future', *Newsletter, the Centre for Management Creativity Network,* July 1999 (quoted in William Tate: *Emergent Business Models,* Council for Excellence in Management and Leadership, Department of Trade and Industry, October 2000)

Appendix 1
About the Audit's Designer

William Tate, MA, FCIPD, FRSA, MCIM, is a freelance organisation consultant and writer. He is the designer of a number of other Cambridge Strategy audits.

Formerly British Airways' Head of Human Resources Strategy & Planning, since 1991 he has run Prometheus Consulting, a practice specialising in strategic human resource management, organisation development, change and learning. He is also a director of Conduct Becoming, a consultancy specialising in corporate social responsibility (CSR), governance and business ethics.

William consults and runs workshops on strategic HR, management and organisation development, and CSR. He is also a visiting member of faculty on City University's Executive MBA programme.

He can be contacted on:

Tel: +44 (0)1252 792322
bill.tate@prometheus-consulting.com
bill.tate@ConductBecoming.com
www.organisational-leadership.com

Other publications by William Tate

- **'Linking development with business'** (ch.) in *Leadership in Organisations: Current Issues and Trends* (ed. John Storey). Routledge 2003
- **'Management development'** (ch.) in *Personnel Management* (co-authored with John Storey). Blackwell 2000
- **Becoming a 'Tomorrow's Company' – a story of transformation** (a case study featuring Birmingham Midshires Building Society). The Centre for Tomorrow's Company 1999
- **Building Tomorrow's Company** – booklets accompanying eight-part video series (leadership, communication, measurement, and the key relationships - customers, employees, investors, suppliers, community). BBC for Business 1999
- **Opportunity Through People** - a consultation document on innovation (with Professor John Storey and Professor David Guest) published by the Chartered Institute of Personnel and Development for its members. CIPD 1997

- **Developing Managerial Competence: A Critical Guide to Methods and Materials.** Gower 1995
- **Performance Development Checklists** – for personal organisers. Prometheus 1995
- **Executive-Match** – a senior executive selection planning tool. Prometheus 1994

APPENDIX 2
ABOUT THE PUBLISHER

Business and Management Resources for forward-thinking organisations

Whatever name you give it, your organisation is almost certainly looking for new ways to *outsmart competitors *win and keep customers *develop new products or services *train and motivate staff *cut costs and delays *increase profits.

Cambridge Strategy Publications has a highly-respected - and rapidly-growing - range of management resources to help you do exactly that. Now being used in more than 90 countries around the world, by organisations large and small and in every business sector, CSP's management resources will help you implement change fast in your organisation.

- If you want to measure performance and implement appropriate change in any area of your business - look at our range of self-assessment audits. They cover all aspects of Marketing, Human Resources and Strategic Business Management.
  Visit www.cambridgestrategy.com or contact us at the address below.

- If you want to harness the power of High-Performance Teams, Total Quality, Benchmarking or Project-Based Reengineering - turn to our Portfolios in these areas. Each contains project guides and planners and a range of tools that you can put to work right away.
  Visit www.cambridgestrategy.com or contact us at the address below.

- If you want to share your experience of conducting this audit or get in touch with other organisations who have also used it - try our online audit network.
  Visit www.cambridgestrategy.com/networking or contact us at the address below.

Cambridge Strategy Publications Ltd.
Station Offices
Station Yard
Axminster
Devon. EX13 5PF.
United Kingdom

Tel: +44 (0)1297 631456
Fax: +44 (0)1297 631456
info@cambridgestrategy.com
www.cambridgestrategy.com

Notes

Notes

www.ingramcontent.com/pod-product-compliance
Lightning Source LLC
LaVergne TN
LVHW060213210926
848481LV00008B/2717